Cumberland County
A Brief History

Cumberland County
A Brief History

Roy Parker, Jr.

Raleigh
Division of Archives and History
North Carolina Department of Cultural Resources
1990

Copyright, 1990, by the North Carolina Division of Archives and History

ISBN 0-86526-243-8

Contents

Maps and Illustrations

Foreword

Since 1963 the Historical Publications Section of the North Carolina Division of Archives and History has published a series of short county histories that have proved popular with citizens, teachers, schoolchildren, and tourists. *Cumberland County: A Brief History* brings to eleven the number of titles in this series. It was written by Roy Parker, Jr., who, as editor of the *Fayetteville Times* and other newspapers, has combined a highly successful career in journalism with a profound love for and appreciation of North Carolina's literary, historical, and artistic traditions. A staunch supporter of North Carolina writers, historians, and artists, Mr. Parker has taken an active role in the state's cultural life and organizations, including the presidencies of the North Carolina Literary and Historical Association and the North Carolina Art Society.

In this brief history of Cumberland County he brings the trenchant observations of a journalist to the colorful history of the upper Cape Fear valley. Settled in large part by Scottish Highlanders in the years just before the American Revolution, Cumberland played a key role in the political, commercial, and military life of North Carolina. From the brutal internal war between whigs and tories in the Revolution, to the punishing invasion of William T. Sherman's blue-clad columns in the Civil War, to the establishment of Fort Bragg during the First World War, a military presence in Cumberland has shaped the county's history in ways unlike almost any other place in North Carolina. Roy Parker's spirited account of Cumberland County captures that unique heritage.

Robert M. Topkins edited the manuscript and saw the book through press. Trudy Rayfield encoded the manuscript and prepared it for typesetting on a microcomputer; Lisa D. Bailey assisted with the proofreading; and Kathleen B. Wyche designed the cover.

Jeffrey J. Crow
Historical Publications Administrator

March, 1990

CHAPTER ONE

The Setting

The 662 square miles of land that encompass present Cumberland County are what remain after three other counties— Moore (760 square miles) in 1784, Harnett (607 square miles) in 1855, and Hoke (382 square miles) in 1911—were carved from it. Cumberland's story is shaped by its natural setting. The geographic backdrop of the county's history includes the Cape Fear River and its many tributaries, the fertile sandy soils and deep forests of the coastal plain, and the unique pine-and-scrub-oak landscape of the Carolina Sandhills.

Early explorers were impressed. In the sixteenth century, Italian explorer Giovanni da Verrazzano described the region's "many faire fields and plains, full of mightie great woods." On the eve of the American Revolution, 250 years later, Janet Schaw, an English visitor to the upper Cape Fear region, was equally eloquent. She wrote: "Nothing can be finer than the banks of this river; a thousand beauties both of the flowery and sylvan tribe hang over it and are reflected from it with additional lustre."

The Cape Fear, Cumberland's principal waterway, was navigable by shallow-draft vessels for 150 miles inland from its mouth. For more than 200 years it was the favored artery for trade and travel. More than thirty other creeks, streams, and smaller tributaries are in present-day Cumberland. Reflecting their early importance, several of them were designated with "white man" names either before or soon after the county was established. The Lower Little River and Rockfish Creek—named by the 1730s—were navigable by rafts and small boats. These streams were ideal sites for small dams, by which water could be utilized to turn the wheels of water mills. Mill sites were major attractions for early settlers. Colonial governments encouraged the establishment of gristmills and sawmills. In the first half of the nineteenth century these waterpower sites supported the most extensive cotton textile factory district in North Carolina. An 1883 survey of waterways in Cumberland County enumerated more than fifty available sites for waterwheels. Water mills were the genesis of Cumberland County's three major communities—Fayetteville, Hope Mills, and Spring Lake. Among such streams were Cross Creek, Carvers Creek, Willis Creek, and Newberry's (later Grays) Creek, which flowed into the Cape Fear from the west, and Lord's Creek and Lock's Creek, which entered the Cape Fear from the east.

The area of Cumberland comprises two geographic land types—the larger portion of the coastal plain in the east and south and the Carolina Sandhills in the west and north. The coastal plain includes typical clay-and-sandy-loam soils, productive for grain and other crops and easily turned into pasture, with rainfall averaging 40 inches a year and a growing season of hot summers and mild winters. Elevations are less than 100 feet above sea level east of the Cape Fear and seldom exceed 250 feet on the west. A distinctive geographic phenomenon of this area are the egg-shaped "Carolina bays," sandy depressions, often water-filled, that have evoked speculation about their origin since earliest days. The Carolina Sandhills, a land of pine trees, scrub oak, wire grass, and deep sandy soils, was a new sort of place to earliest explorers. A 1671 map denoted the "Pine Plains."

As in every place, early visitors to the upper Cape Fear were on the lookout for gold and other precious metals. But the primary money resource of the area turned out to be the pine tree. The pine sent a large taproot through the sand to the clay beneath and a huge, sturdy trunk straight into the air. Its soft, easily milled wood was a basic building resource. Moreover, it was also the source of large supplies of turpentine, rosin, pitch, and tar—commodities known in the eighteenth century as naval stores. These vital products, shipped and stored in barrels, were colonial North Carolina's most important export. Throughout Cumberland's history, pine forests have represented the county's most vital economic resource and have remained the bedrock of the local economy into the twentieth century.

Prehistory, Native Peoples

For thousands of years before European settlers came to the Cape Fear River valley, the region's streams and forests were home to native peoples. Generations of amateur collectors and professional archaeologists have discovered and preserved evidence of their presence. Projectile points, stone tools, bone scrapers, and shards of clay pottery in a variety of styles have been found, representing all the periods of prehistoric culture in North Carolina. These periods extend back 12,000 years, and materials from each of them—Paleo-Indian (12,000-8000 B.C.), Archaic (8000-1200 B.C.), and Early and Late Woodland (1200 B.C.-A.D. 1700)—have been unearthed in the county.

By the time Europeans arrived, distinct tribal groups roamed or lived in the area, hunted, farmed, and buried their dead. These people were generally associated with the language group known as Souian. A dozen distinct groups of such people have been identified within a 100-mile radius of the area that is now Cumberland County. While archaeologists have yet to find specific evidence of European contact with any natives in the area, they have uncovered abundant evidence of prehistoric native life. Artifacts associated with native American life have been observed at more than 100 sites in the county. Many others known to artifact collectors are unrecorded.

Significant marks on the land left by native peoples are the remains of Woodland-period "burial mounds," sites in which skeletons and associated artifacts reveal striking details of prehistoric culture. These mounds appear to be unique to the southern coastal plain. One such mound apparently was excavated by an amateur archaeologist in 1860. Two others, found near Hope Mills, were investigated by a professional scientist as early as 1883. In 1910 an archaeologist excavated several mounds near Hope Mills; this was one of the earliest excavations in the state to be professionally reported. In 1915 amateur archaeologists found "arrow heads, copper ornaments, and bits of pottery" in a mound south of Little Rockfish Creek.

Careful archaeological work in the 1960s uncovered the most noteworthy such native cemetery, the "McLean Mound" east of the Cape Fear near Fayetteville. Remains indicating 268 distinct burials were found, along with stone pipes, points, pottery, and stone tools. Radiocarbon dating of charcoal found among the bones revealed that the mound was constructed about A.D. 970, plus or minus 110 years. A nearby settlement site named "Breece

Village" also produced pottery shards, hearths, and stone fragments. The mound and the settlement site are named for the present owners of the land on which they are found.

Although there is no archaeological or documentary evidence that native peoples inhabited the area of present Cumberland County at the time of initial European exploration, the county's present population includes a significant number of people who identify themselves as the descendants of native Americans. Most of these people are associated with the Lumbee or Tuscarora (both modern names) population that resides principally in Robeson County. The 1980 census enumerated 3,900 such people, most of whom resided in the East Fayetteville district.

Underscoring the very old link between these people and the area, the first listing of Cumberland County's taxables, made in 1755, includes a man with an Indian family name. Major Lockaleer (now commonly spelled Locklear) was listed along with ten other people under the "mulattoe" heading. Early censuses often made no distinction between people of mixed ancestry who were not slaves and native Americans who may have adopted European customs and culture.

Settlement

Settlement of the upper Cape Fear River is part of the larger story of growth in the Carolina colony during the eighteenth century. It is a story of individuals and families making their way up rivers and through forests to begin a new life in a wilderness by carving out farms and pastures.

In the 1720s, following the subduing of the Tuscarora Indians and settlement of the lower Cape Fear at Brunswick and "New Town" (later Wilmington), royal governments and land specu-lators promoted settlement along the upper reaches of the river. Land grants in this area in the early 1730s went mainly to land speculators from as far away as Edenton or Bertie precincts in the Albemarle section, or to royal land agents eager to entice settlers to "take up" acreage. Some settlers did not wait or bother with the niceties of grants or deeds. They simply pushed up the river, picked out a likely tract of land, and settled.

Some of the earliest holders of land grants in present Cumberland were Samuel Swann, Thomas Hart, Hugh Campbell, William Forbes, James Innes (a royal land agent), Thomas Lock, John Brooks, William Blocker, Richard Richardson, William

Russell, and Thomas Matthews. By 1734 enough settlers or grant holders were in the area, especially below the mouth of Rockfish Creek, for Bladen Precinct to be carved from the backcountry of the Cape Fear settlement. The formal designation of a new jurisdiction typically prompted a new surge of settlement.

The settlers came in three general streams. The first was up the Cape Fear River itself. Another came from the already settled Albemarle area. The third, beginning in the early 1740s, was in the form of an outmigration from Pennsylvania and the Chesapeake by way of the Great Wagon Road southwestward through Virginia and the Carolina piedmont; this tide of settlement swelled to a flood in the 1750s.

The upper Cape Fear experienced a distinctive migration peopled by Highland Scots. Unlike other settlers, the Highland Scots came directly from their homeland in the British Isles to begin a new life in the backcountry. They often arrived in groups from Scotland, having been recruited there. At first they arrived in small numbers, but on the eve of the American Revolution their numbers swelled to a point that the British crown became alarmed at Scotland's loss of population.

The first Scots known to have settled in present Cumberland County were known as the "thirty-niners." This group, consisting of "several Scotch gentlemen and several poor people," departed Argyllshire aboard a vessel known as the *Thistle* on June 6, 1739, and arrived in the lower Cape Fear on the following September 23. They immediately journeyed up the river and took possession of land granted them by North Carolina's royal governor, Gabriel Johnston, himself a Scotsman. About two dozen individuals and families from among this group of settlers have been identified as recipients of land grants in the 1740s. Many of their family names are still familiar at the present time. For the most part, these people settled in the district later known as "the Bluff," along both sides of the Cape Fear about four miles south of the Lower Little River. Some were forewarned of the wildness of the region. A Scot seafarer whose relatives were among the settlers had written a year earlier his conclusion that North Carolina was "remarkable for knaves and villains!" Later settlers pushed farther up the Cape Fear, the Little River, Rockfish Creek, and the area between the mouth of Rockfish Creek and the smaller "Cross Creek" stream a few miles north. The Scots mingled with a flood of settlers arriving from the north and west, people known as "Scotch-Irish"—Lowland Scots whose ancestors had fled to Ulster in the north of Ireland. There were also Philadelphia Quakers; Europeans with names like DeBrutz, Dukemineer, and Martinleer; Irishmen; Londoners; and Lowland Scots from Glasgow, as well as second-generation North Carolinians from the Albemarle region.

So rapid was the stream of settlement in the backcountry that Anson Precinct was formed in 1750 from portions of Bladen Precinct west of present-day Hoke and Cumberland counties. By then, the area that was to become Cumberland was sprinkled with scores of farms and pastures. The big waterwheels of a few gristmills and sawmills were turning; a few merchants operated rough warehouse-stores at strategic locations. Tiny settlements had sprung up, notably at the mouth of Rockfish Creek or beside well-settled trading paths along which cattle and backcountry products such as grain, naval stores, and lumber moved toward the lower Cape Fear, and along these paths came a steady stream of fortune-seekers and settlers. To serve this area and promote even more growth, the colonial government was ready to carve out yet another precinct from the backcountry of Bladen.

Colonial Days

Formation

The 1754 colonial assembly, meeting in Wilmington, carved Cumberland County from the backcountry of Bladen Precinct. At that time the new county consisted of more than 2,400 square miles, an area twice the size of present Rhode Island. The county's original southern boundary began at the mouth of Cross Creek on the Cape Fear and ran southwest at a 45-degree angle. When the colonial assembly in 1762 chartered the town of Campbellton on 100 acres just south of the creek's mouth, it annexed the tract to Cumberland. In 1764 and 1789 there were other additions from Bladen, and the present southern boundary essentially was fixed.

The royal government named the new county for William Augustus, duke of Cumberland, soldier son of King George II, who at the time was England's most popular public figure and military hero. The king had pleased colonists by dispatching to North America British troops to protect frontier settlements from marauding Indians. His son's name was being applied to mountain ranges and passes, rivers, and frontier forts that later became towns. Historians frequently mention the irony of the name affixed to a jurisdiction in which settlers from the Highlands of Scotland were numerous, inasmuch as the duke commanded the British army that defeated rebel Highlanders at the fateful battle of Culloden (1746) and was known in the Highlands as "Butcher Billy."

Population

The first enumeration of Cumberland citizenry came in 1755, within months of the county's founding, when new sheriff Hector McNeill and his listers reported as residents 302 white males, 11 "mulattoes" by family name, and "63 [unnamed] Negroes." Reflecting the great size of the jurisdiction and the scattered nature of settlement, the report estimated that there were "Nigh thirty taxables [white males aged sixteen or above and their slaves] more in sd County who have not Given in their list of Taxables." Subsequent counts of Cumberland's taxables revealed 542 white males in 1760, 870 in 1763, and 1,109 in 1765. A report from the latter year enumerated 866 white men and 366 blacks and mulattoes, both male and female. In 1768 the count of taxables totaled 1,179. Because of the peculiarities of colonial record-taking, the figures do not include white females. By 1790, when the United States government conducted its first national census, Cumberland County's total population had climbed to 8,671. Local historians have concluded that of the 302 white males listed in the first list of taxables, 42 lived in what is now Moore County, 82 in what is now Harnett County. A majority of these people had Scottish Highlander surnames. One local historian has asserted that about a third of the total Cumberland list included such names.

Government, Courthouse, County Seat

The government of the new county, the colonial "Court of Pleas & Quarter Sessions," got right down to business. It consisted of approximately a dozen justices of the peace, principally property owners, named by the royal governor with the concurrence of the Executive Council. The records of this body are a major source for the history of Cumberland County in the colonial period.

The court met every three months ("Quarter Sessions") to conduct a wide range of business still familiar in courthouses—approving deeds, wills, and estate divisions and trying civil suits. In addition, it possessed extensive regulatory powers over roads, ferries, gristmills, apprentices, and guardians; named standard keepers, "stray masters," constables, jurors, tax listers, a "venduemaster," and commodity inspectors; recommended to the governor candidates for the office of sheriff; approved cattle brands; designated poor citizens eligible for grants from the "parish tax";

and excused paupers and cripples from paying county taxes. Records of the proceedings of the Cumberland County Court of Pleas & Quarter Sessions begin in October, 1755.

By January, 1756, a meeting place for the court was in use near the mouth of Lower Little River on land belonging to Thomas Armstrong (d. 1765). The place was sometimes referred to as "Choffington" (properly "Chaffering Town," from *chaffer*, meaning to bargain, haggle, or bandy). More often, it was known simply as "the courthouse." It was located near the ferry of John Brown (d. before 1765), a convenience available at no charge to people with court business. In April, 1756, the court levied a tax of 4 pence per taxable for law books and an additional 4 pence per taxable as a means of furnishing the courthouse "with proper conveniences for the magistrates." The last court at Chaffering Town was held in the summer of 1763, after which time the seat of government became the brand-new town of Campbellton at the mouth of Cross Creek. Complaints concerning inadequacies in the Campbellton site led to petitions to abandon it in favor of the Cross Creek settlement.

Settlement Patterns

The earliest settlers, especially the Scots who came directly across the Atlantic, claimed grants and acquired land along both sides of the Cape Fear River and up its tributaries. McNeills, McAllisters, and others from the 1739 group of Highland immigrants settled in abundance near "the Bluff," a district of rolling high ground east of the Cape Fear and south of Lower Little River. There in 1758 the first Presbyterian congregation, presently known as Bluff Church, met with its new minister, the Reverend Hugh Campbell. The importance of Lower Little River is evident in the fact that Cumberland's first county seat was located at its confluence with the Cape Fear, where a ferry was in operation.

Other settlers had pushed up the Cape Fear (McLendon's Creek in present Moore County was already named when Cumberland was established). A considerable waterway several miles south of Lower Little River also was settled by the 1750s, with the Carver and Evans families predominating; it was named Carvers Creek by 1756. A 1750s settlement at the mouth of Rockfish Creek was important enough to be mentioned specifically as a possible site for an official town. A group of Quakers—

among them the Thames, Dunn, and Newberry families—settled south of Rockfish Creek in the area of present-day Grays Creek. The creek itself was previously known as Newberry's. By 1749 Dunns Meeting House was mentioned in church records, but it was discontinued about 1760. Several families from this congregation later became members of the Cape Fear Baptist Church, which was established by 1770. John Copeland was so frequently identified with the sect that deeds refer to him as "the Baptist."

In the interior near tributaries of Rockfish Creek, the east-west trading route known as the "Yadkin Road" was popular with settlers arriving from both east and west. A portion of this route on what is now the Hoke County line was called the "Long Street." Alexander McKay (d. 1769) was an early settler there. The arrival of other families enabled the Reverend Hugh Campbell to establish Long Street Presbyterian congregation there in 1766.

Cross Creek

Cumberland County's most important and enduring settlement sprang up beside Cross Creek, a small, strategically located stream that empties into the Cape Fear River halfway between Lower Little River and Rockfish Creek. Early land grants in the area went to Hugh Campbell, John Russell, Thomas Hart, John Gray, John Brooks, and James Pugh. Early grants for land on the east side of the Cape Fear opposite Cross Creek went to Peter Lord, Michael Blocker, and Leonard Lock.

Merchants from Wilmington were especially interested in the area. By 1756 Richard Lyon (d. 1774) and his partner Hugh Fullerton had erected a rough "store-house" on the river a mile below the mouth of Cross Creek at a spot known as "Springhill." The trading post, stocked with goods from the family's Wilmington warehouses, sought connections with the new Moravian settlement near present-day Winston-Salem. Lyon and Fullerton invited the enterprising newcomers to use the Springhill landing as their doorway to Wilmington's stores and docks. This so-called "Moravian Connection" along the well-settled path connecting Cross Creek with the backcountry would endure for 100 years.

A mile from the mouth of Cross Creek, at a point near the creek, a road leading toward the western Yadkin settlements intersected with a north-south road that connected the older Albemarle section with Wilmington. John Newberry (d. 1771), a

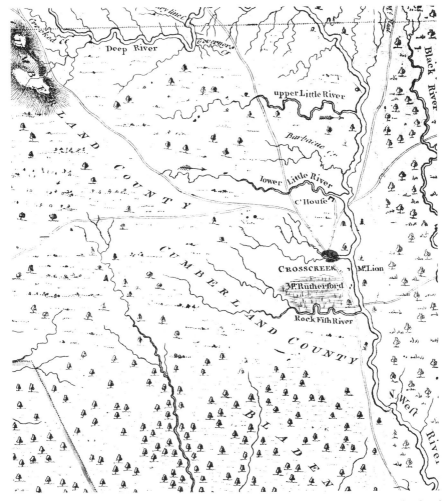

In this detail from a map drawn by John Abraham Collet in 1770, Cumberland County and the village of "Crosscreek" are clearly discernible. From Map Collection, Archives, Division of Archives and History.

Pennsylvania Quaker millwright and taverner who had previously resided on the Pee Dee River to the west, purchased the spot in 1754 and erected a gristmill by the following year. Water still flows over a dam at this genesis site of the place that later became Fayetteville. In 1760 Newberry began settling portions of the tract that embraced most of present-day downtown Fayetteville.

Purchasers of this land were the earliest residents of the Cross Creek settlement. John Walsh (or Welsh) was an early sawmill operator. John Wilcox (1728-1792) and Thomas Hadley (d. 1781?) established a busy mercantile store and another mill just below Newberry's at a crossing by a "Cool spring." Robert Bennerman came upriver from Wilmington, opened a tavern at the Little River court settlement, and later moved to Cross Creek. By the 1760s his ordinary was a popular meeting place. It was located at the intersection presently known as "Liberty Point." Other buyers of Newberry lots in the years before 1763 included John Stevens, the owner of a gristmill; Richard Lyon, who moved his mercantile operation from Springhill in 1760; James and Matthew Porterfield, merchant-innkeepers; John Brownlow, "gent."; Henry Negley (or Neglee), a merchant; John Stevenson, a tailor; Phillip Raiford and Alexander McKay, planters; John Hales (or Hailes), a shoemaker and tavern keeper; John Dobbin, a brewer; James Dyer, a tanner; Joseph Howard, a "doctor of physic"; and Isaiah Parvisol, John Kindell, Patrick Coleman, and Sam Goodman, who were innkeepers or taverners. Of the more than 100 land transactions in the Cross Creek settlement that were recorded during the eleven years following Newberry's 1754 purchase, ninety-six occurred in the 1760-1765 period. A total of seventy-five people have been identified with the Cross Creek settlement by 1765. Two thirds of these people settled there between 1760 and 1765.

At that time the colonial assembly was pressed to charter an official town in which backcountry trade would be encouraged by government-sponsored warehouses and inspectors and facilitated by the services of millers, butcher-tanners, merchandising stores, and taverns. In 1760 a committee that included Richard Lyon was instructed to assess Cross Creek and Rockfish Creek as possible sites. It specifically rejected both and instead recommended a 100-acre tract directly on the river at the mouth of Cross Creek, part of the lands of John Russell (d. 1761). The town chartered in 1762 was named Campbellton, probably for John Campbell (ca. 1700-1781) of Bertie County, an influential planter-politician and friend of the colonial governor. The county court quickly removed from Chaffering Town to Campbellton, and a courthouse and a jail were erected in the latter place by 1763.

While the name Campbellton persisted, the speculative spot never matched the village already well established a mile away. The Campbellton charter actually embraced the Cross Creek settlement by allowing anyone within a mile of the courthouse to vote for town officials and later for a town member of the assembly, thus removing another incentive for growth at the riverside site. The Cross Creek settlement grew steadily as a commercial center after 1760. A bridge spanned the creek by 1765, connecting "the King's Road" (present Green Street) and the "old Street" (present Old and Bow streets). Both sides of the settlement's streets were increasingly crowded with dwellings, stores, and mills.

Appropriately, the first mention of Cross Creek in a newspaper (Edenton and Wilmington) had to do with commerce. A 1765 notice announced the dissolution of the mercantile combination of Hadley & Wilcox. In 1767 thirty-six businessmen signed a petition requesting that the courthouse and jail be moved to Cross Creek, "whose situation is Healthy Airy and dry & every conveniency immediately at hand." The official site at Campbellton, in contrast, was said to be "surrounded by so many Swamps & Morasses" and lacking "a House of Entertainment." By 1770, when the royal governor commissioned official maps of the principal places in the colony, Cross Creek was depicted with more than forty structures, including mills, a brewery, a tannery, and the county jail (but not the courthouse). Campbellton was not mapped.

In 1772 many of the same businessmen who had signed the 1767 petition asked the governor to alter the original charter of Campbellton to bar "transient persons, Boatmen Waggoners and other Laborers" from voting in village elections. The charter was so altered. As the American Revolution approached, the town bustled with growth as new waves of Scottish immigrants and people from other parts of the colony settled in Cumberland.

A rare contemporary glimpse of Cross Creek and Campbellton and an appropriate summation of the colonial history of the two towns is from the pen of William Bartram (1739-1823), a renowned naturalist, who as a young man in the 1760s may have worked as a clerk in a Cross Creek store and visited Campbellton just prior to the Revolution. He later described the towns' beginnings and early growth, though he greatly exaggerated Campbellton's size:

. . . enterprising men . . . built mills, which drew people to the place [Cross Creek], and there observing eligible situations for other profitable improvements, bought lots and erected tenements, where they exercised mechanic arts, as smiths, wheelwrights, carpenters, coopers, tanners, &c. And at length merchants were encouraged to adventure and settle: in short,

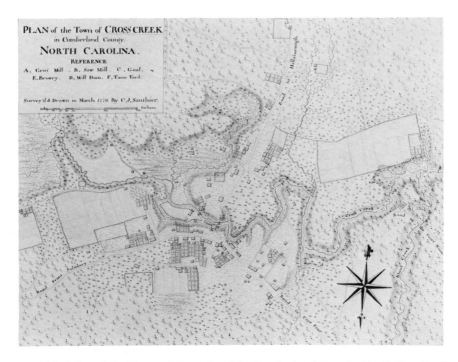

This "Plan of the Town of Cross Creek in Cumberland County, North Carolina" was surveyed and drawn by cartographer Claude Joseph Sauthier in March, 1770. It identifies major man-made features of the early town. Map reproduced by permission of the British Library.

within eight or ten years, from a grist-mill, saw-mill, smith-shop and a tavern, arose a flourishing commercial town, the seat of government of the county of Cumberland. . . . When I was here about twenty years ago [ca. 1760], this town [Campbellton] was marking out its bounds, and there were then about twenty habitations; and now there are above a thousand houses [*sic*], many wealthy merchants, and respectable public buildings, a vast resort of inhabitants and travellers, and continual brisk commerce by waggons, from the back settlements, with large trading boats, to and from Wilmington. . . .

Notable Colonial Personalities

Among leading figures in the colonial history of Cumberland County not otherwise mentioned were the following men:

ALEXANDER MCALLISTER (d. 1795). Original "Bluff" settler, legislator, Revolutionary War leader, early slave owner. Many black families share his Scottish surname and those of his neighbors—the McNeills, Eliots, and Smiths.

ROBERT ROWAN (ca. 1738-1798). Perhaps the county's leading citizen of the eighteenth century. In Cross Creek settlement by the early 1760s, sheriff, legislator, Revolutionary War leader; in "Sons of Liberty" by 1770. Circulated statement known as the "Liberty Point Resolves," signed at Cross Creek in June, 1775. Stepfather of Congressman William Barry Grove.

THOMAS RUTHERFORD (d. 1782). Owner of Tweedside, a river plantation east of the Cape Fear, by 1756. A kinsman of Wilmington merchant-speculators, a clerk of court, a militia officer. Captured as a loyalist at the battle of Moores Creek Bridge in 1776. His widow, Jane, recovered confiscated lands.

FARQUHARD CAMPBELL (ca. 1730-1808). Born in Scotland. In colony of North Carolina by 1750s; a large landowner at "Bluff" and Cross Creek; a justice of the peace by 1756; legislator; captain in militia that marched against Regulators; surveyor of Campbellton, to which his name was long attached; briefly a loyalist during the Revolution; a prisoner at Moores Creek. After the war he recovered his prewar status and served in legislature. He owned fifty slaves in 1790.

ROBERT COCHRAN (d. 1786). A Pennsylvania Quaker and tanner. Bought Newberry's mill, 1765. A prosperous merchant, justice of the peace, legislator. His son, Robert (1773-1842), removed to Wilmington in 1807 to serve as United States collector of customs there.

ROBERT HOGG (1729-1805). Lived in Wilmington and Hillsborough; a merchant-landowner whose brother first acquired property at Cross Creek in 1768. By the time of the Revolution, he vied with Robert Cochran as its major landowner.

HECTOR MCNEILL (d. 1768), DUNCAN MCNEILL (d. 1793), DUGALD MCNEILL, DUNCAN CAMPBELL. Scottish settlers in 1739 and colonial county officials.

THOMAS GIBSON (d. 1762), WALTER GIBSON. Brothers, planter-merchants, owners of a gristmill, keepers of a ferry on Lower Little River, earliest members of colonial assembly.

MICHAEL BLOCKER (d. 1761). Early settler east of Cape Fear; family operated ferries, mills. Other colonial settlers in this area were Leonard Lock and Peter Lord.

Black People

From the 63 slaves and 11 "mullatoes" (free blacks) mentioned in the 1755 list of Cumberland County taxables, the number of black people steadily increased to more than 2,100 by 1790, the year of the first census of the United States. The first black person mentioned by name in the county records was "one Negro girl named Pennallopy," who in 1758 was deeded to James Muse from the estate of his late father. Free black citizens were mentioned for the first time in 1758 by a county record that referred to a "boy named Antone," who had been freed from an indenture. In that same year a free Negro named Gideon Cumbo hired a lawyer in an unsuccessful attempt to be declared insolvent by the county court.

Most black people worked as slaves, usually as field hands in tobacco or in turpentine-related or tar-making enterprises. Some blacks apparently were artisans, blacksmiths, or coopers. "Bob," a twenty-two-year-old slave cooper, "High African born and bred," brought the large sum of £120 when sold to merchant Robert Adam in 1790. Some slaves were trusted enough to be granted licenses to carry guns. William Dawson, Esq., received such a license for his slave, Jeffrey, in 1758, and Robert Woods, a slave of Hector McNeill, was licensed in 1764. Free blacks served as boatmen, draymen, or servants. Children of mixed parents often were apprenticed to white families, and there were court fights to prevent such children from being kept as slaves. Colonial records of Cumberland contain about sixty references to slaves or free blacks. A total of 104 slave sales were recorded in the forty-five years prior to 1790. According to the 1790 census, twelve slave owners, including four in Cross Creek, owned twenty or more slaves.

The Economy

The colonial agricultural economy was based on livestock, Indian corn, wheat and other grains, and forest products. In the 1770s tobacco became important. Tanneries, gristmills, sawmills, and warehouses sprang up to serve this agricultural base. The production of tar ("naval stores") was of growing importance in the latter years of the period. The first tobacco inspectors were named at Cross Creek in 1772. In 1775 an inspector was named for tar, pitch, turpentine, flaxseed, beef, pork, butter, indigo, "etc. etc."

Statistics on crops are rare, but the county records are studded with mentions of livestock—beef and milk cows, horses, and especially hogs. There appears to have been some long-distance trading. Stephen Gilmore in 1763 sold "22 head of cattle running at large in or about 10 miles of Frederick Town in Maryland." Most such commerce was local, however, with only tobacco and naval stores serving as cash crops. In 1771-1772, 340 hogsheads of tobacco were stored in Cross Creek warehouses; 474

were stored there in 1772-1773, and 50 were reported in 1775. The inventory of the estate of Thomas Rutherford, a substantial planter, included 94 hogsheads of tar ready for sale in Wilmington.

Occupations

Approximately 170 individuals whose occupations were other than planter or farmer have been identified in the colonial-era records of Cumberland County. They included 31 merchants, 30 millers, 13 blacksmiths, 19 carpenters, 17 coopers, 12 tailors, 9 weavers, 7 shoemakers ("cordweiners"), and 4 hat makers. Other occupations with at least one practitioner in the county were: trader, brewer, bricklayer, brickmaker, britches maker, joiner, tanner-merchant, miller-merchant, sawyer, millwright, wagoner, turner, victualler, wheelwright, rope maker, and wool comber.

Taverns

"Places of entertainment," a name for taverns and ordinaries, customarily public rooms attached to dwellings, were the colonial equivalent of television, fast-food shops, a night on the town, motels, and political clubhouses. Cumberland County was rich in them. In 1756, its first full year of business, the county court licensed ten such places. The following year it licensed a total of fifteen tavern keepers, eleven of whom were newcomers. Among the latter group was Mary Jones, the county's first female entrepreneur on record. Mary Brown and Catherine Thornton held tavern licenses in 1764.

The number of tavern licenses averaged a dozen yearly until the Revolution, peaking at nineteen in 1774. Several of the facilities were familiar places. Alexander McKay's, licensed in 1759 and still going strong in 1778, was near the meetinghouse of Long Street Presbyterian Church. When the Reverend Hugh McAden visited and preached at McKay's in January, 1756, he reported that, following the service, the audience "stayed around the Tavern all night drinking and carousing."

Perhaps the most noted establishment was that of Stephen Gilmore (1735-1816), which was licensed in 1772 and still operating in 1788. A map of the period showing distances from Wilmington to other places in North Carolina depicts "Gilmore's house" four miles north of Cross Creek. Gilmore proudly gave his occupation as "innkeeper." Tavern business was naturally centered in the settlements. There were at least three at Chaffering Town, the earliest court site. Robert Bennerman, a Wilmington tavern keeper, opened an ordinary there, then moved to Cross Creek. The early taverners of that village have been mentioned. There were six village licensees in 1774. Later colonial innkeepers were Lewis Barge (d. 1809), Archy McEacheren, Lewis Bowel (d. 1795), Aaron Verdie, and George Fletcher (d. 1781).

Revolution

The period of the American Revolution was a time of divided loyalties in Cumberland County. A considerable portion of Cumberland's people—especially the Highland Scots—were either staunchly loyal to the British crown or indifferent to the war. The county served primarily as a granary and supply depot for military columns and for the war effort generally. It was often swept by rumors of impending invasions, but actual military activity— which was marked by sporadic acts of violence between patriots and loyalists—occurred only in early 1776 and during 1781, the final year of the war. In February, 1781, Charles, Lord Cornwallis and his British army marched through Cumberland County on their way to Guilford Court House, where a pivotal battle took place on March 15. Retreating from that battle, Cornwallis passed through Cross Creek on April 7. There followed partisan fighting between loyalists and local patriots. This confused activity culminated in a raid by a tory band on August 14 into Cross Creek while the county court was in quarterly session. The tory force, led by David Fanning, temporarily held several of the patriot leaders as prisoners.

The county was also the home of a number of active patriots. On June 30, 1775, at a rally in Cross Creek, sixty-nine of them signed "the association," later called the "Liberty Point Resolves," a document named for a road intersection (and tavern) at which the gathering took place. Participants in the rally vowed to "go forth and be ready to sacrifice our lives and fortunes to secure her [the county's] freedom and safety." The leader in this episode was

Robert Rowan, the county's most noted colonial personality. He and militia colonel Alexander McAllister, likewise a member of the provincial congress, were the county's major patriot leaders. Other key figures were militia lieutenant colonel Ebenezer Folsom (d. 1788), who was commended for his "spirit and activity" in suppressing tories and commandeering supplies in his home county (and later also asked to curb his zeal when he was alleged to be oppressing patriots as well); John Blocker, who with Folsom was a "firearms procurer" for the provincial congress; James Emmett, active colonel in the militia and later legislator; and young Arthur Council, killed in 1777 while an officer in the Sixth North Carolina Regiment.

Cumberland lacks a thorough study of those who served in the Continental forces. Several hundred men from the county served either as ordinary soldiers in Continental military units or in loyalist units, in the latter case principally near Charleston, South Carolina. In 1778, for instance, Cumberland's quota for Continental forces was seventy-three men out of a statewide total of 2,648.

Cumberland's most important role in the Revolutionary era was connected with some of the earliest scenes of the war, particularly the days leading up to the battle of Moores Creek Bridge. During this battle, which took place February 27, 1776, a small patriot army defeated a force of loyalist Highland Scots marching from Cross Creek toward Wilmington. The loyalists had rallied at Cross Hill (later known as Carthage) and Cross Creek in response to a summons from the royal governor. According to legend, before they set out from Cross Creek, the loyalists were exhorted by Flora Macdonald, the heroine of rebel Scottish history, who with her family had immigrated to the Cape Fear River valley in 1774 and whose husband, Allan, was among the prisoners taken at Moores Creek.

In those early months of the conflict, many of the county's leading citizens—and hundreds of ordinary people—were either cautious about the patriot cause or openly loyal to the crown. Two county delegates to the First Provincial Congress—Farquhard Campbell and Thomas Rutherford—were subsequently banished as tories, although Campbell rejoined the patriot fold and regained his property. Loyal too were large numbers of ordinary citizens, especially Highland Scots. The county court in 1778 issued orders for "three of four hundred" citizens who were "disaffected to the American cause" to take a prescribed loyalty oath. In that year about one in twenty county taxpayers were charged penalties for failing to take the oath of allegiance to the provincial government, and many others were simply absent or not counted. By 1780, with the system fully operative, fully one third of the taxpayers in some districts were assessed penalties.

An important change unrelated to the war took place in 1778, when the General Assembly gave its assent to the long-sought move of the county court from Campbellton up to the considerable village of Cross Creek. The act combined Campbellton and Cross Creek into a single town, designated as "Lower Campbellton" and "Upper Campbellton" (formerly Cross Creek); specified that the courthouse should be in the latter; and exhorted town officials to lay out new streets "in a regular manner." A new courthouse was promptly erected on newly named "Maiden Lane" and was in use by 1779.

County records suggest that during much of the war, life went on as usual for most of Cumberland's citizens. The signing of loyalty oaths, the naming of "commissioners of confiscated property," and the claims made against some large loyalist estates were new matters punctuating the court records. But there also continued to be much routine business—naming road overseers and patrols, licensing taverns, collecting taxes, ordering bridges built, and repairing jails. There is evidence of raging inflation, a wartime problem as severe as the lack of a stable currency in colonial times. The Revolutionary War gave birth to an enduring place-name in the county: 71st Township was named for a famous Highlander regiment of the British army that marched through the county and later surrendered at Yorktown.

The Golden Decade

The years 1781-1789 were a unique time for Cumberland and a golden, fateful period for Cross Creek. With its new name and a new appearance, the village narrowly missed becoming the capital of the state, then hosted a convention and legislature that ratified the United States Constitution and chartered the University of North Carolina.

The era opened as the Revolutionary War ended—British troops withdrew from Wilmington in November, 1781. A visitor to Cross Creek would recognize it much as before the war: a settlement of gristmills, stores, tanneries, taverns, a jail, and dwellings sprung up willy-nilly beside old colonial trading paths and meandering Cross Creek. The new courthouse stood just up the creekside from Newberry's old mill, now owned by the prosperous merchant-developer Robert Cochran.

Plans were afoot for changes even more momentous. There was talk of establishing a permanent capital of the state. Cross Creek was a candidate. The 1783 legislature set the stage for the town's bid by repeating a 1778 act ordering Cross Creek to be laid out in a "regular and convenient manner," meaning the gridlike pattern of broad streets punctuated by squares—the standard eighteenth-century design for towns. The act also changed the name of the settlement. It would no longer be Cross Creek, or "Upper Campbellton" and "Lower Campbellton." It would be "Fayetteville," one of the first places in the United States named for the young marquis de Lafayette, hero of the Revolution. Seven legislators—none from Cumberland—named by the law met in

July, 1783, and completed their work in a single day, laying out a plan of streets and two squares. Four major streets were named for members of this group—John Hay, James Gillespie, Ambrose Ramsey, and Thomas Person. Seven other men, including longtime residents Robert Cochran, Robert Rowan, and Lewis Barge, were named "directors" to make alterations to accomplish the new plan. Many structures, including a fifteen-year-old jail, were sited on what ultimately became broad streets.

The next assembly in 1784 decisively altered the boundaries of the county outside Fayetteville. It cut off the northwestern portion—nearly 32 percent of the total land area—as a new county and named it for Revolutionary War hero Captain James Moore. Several thousand citizens, including a large proportion of the Highland Scot element in the population, no longer resided in Cumberland.

Meanwhile, the village with the new name continued to grow. A wave of new citizens arrived, among them merchants, artisans, physicians, and former Revolutionary War soldiers. After 1787 Fayetteville was a stop on the circuit of state trial-court judges. As the county seat, it also supported a battery of lawyers. Other, less exalted, people also sought their fortunes in the bustling town— tavern keepers (there were seven in 1788), boatmen, draymen, coopers, free blacks. In 1784 town tax lists named about seventy-five property owners. Six years later, the 1790 census enumerated a town population of more than 270 male adults, more than 1,000 free whites, 34 free blacks, and more than 500 slaves.

Not a full-time citizen but one of the most influential developers of the town was James Hogg, who had inherited from his brother, John Hogg, extensive properties and mercantile establishments in Fayetteville, Wilmington, and Hillsborough. In 1785 Hogg gave the town land for a burying ground, and the following year he donated the site for a new courthouse. That building, erected by the autumn of 1786, was located on the square at the north end of Green Street. With many alterations, it remained in use for 107 years. In 1789 Hogg donated to the town a nearby site for a new jail.

The new courthouse was completed just in time for the 1786 session of the North Carolina General Assembly, which convened in the town in December and met daily in the new building. Fayetteville was showing itself off as a candidate for permanent state capital, but the assembly took no action on that matter. Its major activity was the naming of delegates to attend a convention in Philadelphia in 1787 to consider changes in the Articles of Confederation.

In 1787-1788, as the Philadelphia convention went beyond its mandate and came forth with a new constitution, Fayetteville also faced a fateful decision. The issue of where to locate a permanent capital for North Carolina was coming to a head. A convention to decide whether North Carolina would ratify the handiwork of the Philadelphia conclave gathered in Hillsborough in the summer of 1788. Composed largely of legislators, it debated not only the constitution but also a resolution designating a site for the state capital. Fayetteville had a new lure—a handsome brick building constructed on the square at the south end of Green Street. Its builders named it the "State-House," and a deed for it was rushed to Hillsborough by horseback rider. A 1788 Wilmington newspaper article boosted the town's claim and provided a vivid contemporary view of the place:

Fayetteville's "State-House" (*extreme left*), at which the North Carolina General Assembly convened on several occasions in the late 1780s, was the site at which some 290 delegates assembled in November, 1789, to ratify the United States Constitution on behalf of the state. Engraving from a drawing by M. Horace Say, who presented it to the marquis de Lafayette in 1814. Photograph of engraving courtesy North Carolina Collection, University of North Carolina Library, Chapel Hill.

A traveler who has lately traveled through this state, informs us, that he has no where observed so much public spirit, as in Fayette-Ville. At that place they have lately opened several new roads, and raised a number of new bridges, in order to render the communication with the country more easy and convenient—They have also erected two large and elegant buildings for the accommodation of their courts and the General Assembly.

There is a company formed to make Cross-Creek navigable for boats from the river to the upper town.

All these improvements are carried out by private subscriptions.

This proposed navigation of the Creek, will, as expected, greatly lessen the expense which is occasioned by conveying merchandize and etc. from the landing to the town in waggons as well as add much to the beauty of the place.

In short, it is the opinion of our correspondent, that, considering the situation of Fayette-Ville, so convenient for commanding the trade of an extensive back country, and its other advantages, that it must soon become a place of great consequence, as well as worthy of being the Capital of an extensive state.

It was not to be. The convention first approved a resolution neither to ratify nor reject the proposed United States Constitution (Cumberland's delegates voted in the minority), then recommended a site near Wake Courthouse as the new capital. The 1788 session of the General Assembly met in Fayetteville later that year and used the new building. But it did not rescind the summer decision.

In the last weeks of 1789 the town had one more major role to play in the momentous decade. Both the General Assembly and a second constitutional convention met in the town, the former beginning on November 2. On November 21, after only five days of discussion, the convention delegates ratified the United States Constitution. There was a sad pause when former governor Richard Caswell, the state's most admired Revolutionary War hero, died soon after suffering a stroke while presiding over the state Senate. An elaborate state funeral was hastily organized.

On December 11 the legislature chartered the University of North Carolina. It named the state's first two United States senators. Before adjourning on December 22, it ceded to the federal government the state's western lands—lands that became the state of Tennessee seven years later. Before leaving, the assembly awarded Fayetteville a consolation prize for failing in its bid to be named state capital. It granted the town a "town member" seat in the lower house of the assembly, a privilege that

Cool Spring Place originated as Cool Spring Tavern, which opened its doors to the public in 1789, just in time to serve the delegates who flocked to Fayetteville in November of that year to debate the question of ratifying the United States Constitution. Cool Spring Place, now a lawyer's office, is believed to be the oldest extant structure in Fayetteville and the only surviving building associated with this important gathering. The original 1788 structure may be the core of a later Federal-period enlargement. Photograph courtesy North Carolina Collection.

had been enjoyed for a while prior to 1775 but denied under the Revolutionary War constitution. The assembly met again in Fayetteville in 1790 and 1793 before moving permanently to Raleigh in 1794.

CHAPTER FIVE

The Antebellum Years

The antebellum era—seventy years from the beginning of the new United States to the guns of the Civil War—saw both stability and change. Farming as the chief occupation and slavery as the chief social characteristic marked the entire period. The economy of Cumberland County was notable for the growth of cotton as king of agriculture and for Fayetteville's unsuccessful struggle to become a commercial metropolis.

Despite its modest size, the village of Fayetteville was an important place in a state with few places larger than crossroads. Its antebellum history was typical southern town life, with a full range of commercial and cultural activities. In 1825 it welcomed its namesake, the aged marquis de Lafayette, who made an overnight stop there during a tour of the United States. Virtually destroyed by a great fire in 1831, Fayetteville bounced back to become a commercial center, a battleground of the two-party political system, and the hub of the brief "plank road" age.

Rural Cumberland changed little during the period. A few large landowners, hundreds of small farmers, and thousands of slaves worked to wring a living from fields and forests. Unique in this era were the county's role as an early center of cotton textile manufacture, the contributions of several notable free black personalities in the realms of religion and commerce, and the selection of Fayetteville as the site of a United States arsenal.

Population Perspective

In the eight censuses conducted between 1790 and 1860, the population of Cumberland County grew from 8,671 to 16,369. It

This watercolor of a portion of Fayetteville by British-born artist Charles Catton is believed to have been rendered about 1804, shortly after Catton had concluded a tour of the American South. The scene looks west from the point at which Green Street crosses Cross Creek in downtown Fayetteville. The mill at left is shown on the site of a mill built by John Newberry in 1755-1756, around which the village of Cross Creek evolved. Photograph supplied by the author.

reached 20,000 in 1850 but decreased by 8,000 when Harnett County was formed from portions of northern Cumberland in 1855. Black people accounted for a continually increasing percentage—from 26.1 percent in 1790 to 41.6 percent in 1860. Fayetteville's population totaled 1,529 in 1790, was 3,532 in 1820, and 4,790 in 1860. Black people constituted 45 percent of more of Fayetteville residents until 1860, when they represented 41 percent. Fayetteville remained a village, but its inhabitants constituted an "urban" portion of the total population of Cumberland, which was exceeded only by New Hanover County in total percentage of urban residents.

Politics

Has any period in American history been accompanied by politics more colorful than the years between the founding of the

This detail of a map drawn by Robert H. B. Brazier and published in 1833 by John MacRae (who served as mayor of Fayetteville from 1818 to 1853) shows the configuration of Cumberland County at that time. After 1833 Harnett County was formed from Cumberland (1855), a small portion of Bladen County was annexed to Cumberland (1874), and Hoke County was formed from portions of Cumberland and Robeson counties (1911). From Map Collection, State Archives.

Republic under the Constitution and its sundering by the Civil War? The seasons were marked by activities of famous political figures, the waxing and waning of political parties, notable campaigns, significant elections. Cumberland shared this politics.

Such a survey as this can make only major points about the county's political history. The most notable public men (antebellum politics being an exclusive male preserve) included:

WILLIAM BARRY GROVE (1764-1818). Born in Cross Creek. Stepson of Robert Rowan, the lawyer-entrepreneur. Member of constitutional convention. Federalist congressman, 1791-1802.

JOHN HAY (1757-1809). Born in Belfast, lawyer-developer (a residential section on the escarpment west of Fayetteville known as "Hay-mount" named for him by 1784); legislator; son-in-law of Robert Rowan.

ROBERT STRANGE (1796-1854). Native of Virginia and graduate of Hampden-Sydney College. Studied law under Grove. Legislator; United States senator, 1836-1840; state circuit judge. Author of *Eoneguski, or The Cherokee Chief: A Tale of Past Wars* (1839), the first novel to employ North Carolina as a setting.

JAMES COCHRAN DOBBIN (1814-1857). Born in Fayetteville. Ranks as most significant Cumberland public figure. Graduate of the University of North Carolina, 1832. Lawyer; congressman, 1845-1847; legislator; speaker

Two of the leading politicians to reside in Cumberland County during the antebellum period were Robert Strange (*left*) and James C. Dobbin (*right*). Strange, a native of Virginia, in addition to making his mark as a state legislator, United States senator, and judge, is recognized as the author of the first novel to employ North Carolina as a setting. Dobbin, a native of Fayetteville, is seen as the county's most significant public figure. Artist and date of portrait of Strange unknown; photograph from Albert Barden Photograph Collection, in the possession of the Division of Archives and History; portrait of Dobbin by Eastman Johnson, owned by the Philanthropic Society, University of North Carolina at Chapel Hill.

of North Carolina House of Commons, 1852. Sponsored bill establishing state insane asylum. Made presidential nominating speech for Franklin Pierce. As secretary of navy under Pierce, 1853-1857, presided over steam modernization. Died at home a few months after leaving Washington and eulogized nationwide.

JOHN MACRAE (1793-1880). Fayetteville postmaster, 1818-1853; editor; politician; advocate of internal improvements. Typified antebellum spirit of Fayetteville as bumptious commercial town yearning to be a metropolis. Sponsored sojourn of Robert H. B. Brazier, professional surveyor who prepared 1825 map of town and state. Sons and grandsons important lawyers and public figures.

EDWARD J. HALE (1802-1883). Editor-owner, 1824-1865, of *Fayetteville Observer*; Whig leader, then fiery Confederate. Office destroyed by Sherman's army, 1865. Moved to New York. His sons reestablished the newspaper the year he died.

JAMES SEAWELL. Planter-entrepreneur and politician. Sponsored first steamboat on the Cape Fear and the Cape Fear River bridge. Whig legislator and chairman of Internal Improvements Committee of the House of Commons, 1833-1835. An advocate of railroads in the 1830s. Went bankrupt and removed to Mississippi.

JOHN KELLY (1768-1842). Irish immigrant who arrived in the county by the 1820s. By the 1840s owned large acreages of farmland, town properties, 36 slaves. Leading Roman Catholic. Active in banks, public works, educational projects. An ardent Jacksonian and leader of Democratic party.

DR. BEN ROBINSON (1775-1857). Native of Vermont. Said to have been urged by Thomas Jefferson to remove to North Carolina. Arrived instate in 1805 and served as a leading medical practitioner for fifty years (an early advocate of smallpox vaccination). Longtime chairman of county court. A Jeffersonian, then a Whig. Sons and grandsons were Confederate officers, lawyers, physicians, and politicians.

JOHN WINSLOW (d. 1820). Leader in business and banking, founder of St. John's Episcopal Church; booster of educational and civic causes; state senator, 1815-1819. His son, Warren Winslow (1810-1861), was a leading Democrat of the 1850s, acting governor for a few weeks in 1854, and a three-term congressman, 1855-1861.

HENRY POTTER (1764-1857). Native of Virginia. Named federal judge by Thomas Jefferson in 1802 and remained active for fifty years. Moved to Fayetteville from Raleigh in 1821.

LOUIS D. HENRY (1788-1846). A native of Princeton, New Jersey. Lawyer, mayor of Fayetteville, speaker of North Carolina House of Commons in 1832, Democratic candidate for governor in 1842. Leader in field of internal improvements. Spanish claims commissioner, 1837. A fiery political campaigner who killed Thomas J. Stanly of New Bern in an 1813 duel.

LAUCHLIN BETHUNE (1785-1874). Native of western Sandhills region (presently Hoke County); planter; outspoken Jacksonian legislator; state senator, 1817-1827; congressman, 1831-1833; Democratic party chairman in 1830s and 1840s.

Two other men from Cumberland County served as Speaker of the North Carolina House of Commons: Colonel Thomas Davis in 1809 and Jesse Shepherd in 1856. Among longtime Cumberland legislators, in addition to Lauchlin Bethune, were Neill McNeill, 1815-1823; David McNeill, 1831-1835; and John McKay, eight years between 1788 and 1807.

There were few elective offices, but elections were frequent. Voters balloted for congressmen every two years, presidential electors every four, state legislators every year (every two years after constitutional changes in 1835). They elected two members of the North Carolina House of Commons and one state senator. Until a new state constitution was adopted in 1835, Fayetteville was entitled to elect a "town member" of the House of Commons. After 1835 the governor, previously chosen every year by the legislature, was elected every two years by the voters. In addition, there were annual municipal elections in Fayetteville.

Leaders generally came from the ranks of the well-to-do. Lawyers, merchants, and planters were about equally represented in lists of candidates and party activists. Those classed as activists were roughly divided, too, between town and rural. Free blacks were permitted to participate in elections until 1835, and many did. Voter participation was high. Well over 70 percent of those qualified to vote did so in most elections. More than 800 voted in the first congressional election in 1790. In 1824, 733 qualified citizens voted in the presidential election. That figure rose to 1,562 in 1840 and 2,020 in 1856.

In the early years of the Republic, a political era known as the "First American Party System," Cumberland was a Federalist enclave in a Jeffersonian state. In 1802 five-term Federalist congressman William Barry Grove was defeated and later replaced by an out-of-county Jeffersonian. Men earlier identified with Federalism continued to be elected to legislative seats until the 1820s, long after the party labels had withered away.

With the coming of the "Second American Party System" in the 1820s, Cumberland voters were at first ardent supporters of Andrew Jackson. Thereafter, beginning in the 1830s, they split into sharply delineated Democratic and Whig parties. Although Democrats usually commanded a majority at the polls, nearly every election between 1836 and 1860 was a spirited, hard-fought affair.

In state politics Cumberland was a Democratic stronghold during the period 1836-1850, a time during which the Whigs controlled the state government in Raleigh. The county produced several party leaders, notably Louis D. Henry, the 1842 Democratic candidate for governor. Whig leadership was provided by Edward Jones Hale (1802-1883), editor of the *Fayetteville Observer*, and by Dr. Ben Robinson, who maintained his post on the county court thanks to a Whig legislature that appointed justices of the peace. When Democrats swept to victory in Raleigh in the late 1840s and 1850s, Cumberland provided several of the younger leaders—James C. Dobbin, Warren Winslow, and Jesse Shepherd.

Political campaigns took on many trappings familiar at the present time. There were rallies and parades, newspaper advertisements and broadsides, personal politicking, and speechmaking—often of stupefying length. A well-known campaign menu—barbecue—was already popular. In 1810 a disputed election for town member of the legislature turned in part on charges of undue influence at a political feast hosted by Isaac Hammond, a notable free black barber and militia musician. An affidavit alleged that "[there was] plenty of provender and spirits. They [the celebrants] appeared merry, and there were frequent Huzzas. . . ." The fare included "two shoats roasted and boiled victuals." In the 1840s candidates for governor traveled together to engage in hours-long debates at Fayetteville's Market House.

Despite the hoopla and rhetoric, antebellum politics was not an engine of change. On truly vital issues, there tended to be general agreement. Locally, most leaders of both parties favored so-called "internal improvements" such as a railroad for Fayetteville, improvements to navigation on the Cape Fear River, and other public projects designed to boost the local economy. On the overarching issue, slavery, all vied to be its ardent champion. As historian Harry Watson has written in his study of the Second American Party System in Cumberland: "The end result of party formation was a political system that expressed deep divisions within each community but which left the basic patterns of economic and social relations undisturbed."

County Government

The form of county government changed little between 1790 and 1860. The Court of Pleas and Quarter Sessions of colonial days continued, a gathering of appointive justices of the peace named by the legislature and comprised of men from the more well-to-do class. The sheriff and court clerk became full-time officers. The sheriff was an elected official in the 1850s. Tax assessments and collections customarily were made by "captain's districts," later townships. Soon after 1800 the county met its growing obligation to the destitute by establishing a poorhouse and an almshouse. The census of 1860 listed eighteen people as residents of the Cumberland poorhouse.

The relative size of government can be deduced from tax statistics. In 1803 the county collected a total of only $649 for the state. Of that amount, $77.00 came from Fayetteville and $56.00 from a tax on taverns, the largest such figure in the state. In 1815 the assessed valuation of property in the county was $1.3 million in land and $929,000 in slaves. Two years later the county collected only $2,718 from this base. Cumberland usually ranked in the top half-dozen counties in tax collections. Town property accounted for about a third of the total property valuation. In 1860 the county collected $10,500 annually, including $3,234 for a special poor tax.

Town Government

Although it remained a village even by contemporary standards, Fayetteville was nonetheless as large an inland town as the state boasted in these years. Its government was appropriately complex. Governance was set by legislative acts culminating in a 1794 law "for the better regulation of Fayetteville." Elected officials included seven commissioners chosen from geographic wards and a "magistrate of police" (mayor after 1857) elected annually. These officials regulated the activities of slaves and free Negroes, enacted fire-protection measures, controlled taverns and other public places, and set rules to regulate the market portion of the Town Hall (Market House). Each ward had a volunteer patrol to enforce regulations concerning racial matters. Subsequently a "Director of Patrols" was employed.

A formidable list of stipend-paid officials identifies government responsibilities. In 1851 the following officers were receiving stipends: a town clerk, a treasurer, a tax collector, a special justice, a printer, a constable, a market clerk, and directors of patrols in upper Fayetteville and lower Fayetteville. By 1857 the town payroll had been shuffled and apparently shortened. It then included one individual who was at the same time constable, director of patrols, lamp tender, standard keeper, and street

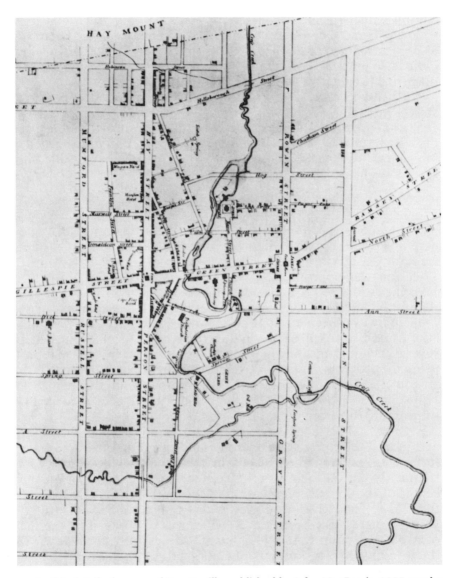

In this detail of a map of Fayetteville published by John MacRae in 1825 can be seen the town's principal thoroughfares and the locations of some of its noteworthy buildings. From Map Collection, State Archives.

commissioner (at an annual salary of $525); four town guards at $250 each; and a chief fire warden and seven assistants. There was also a part-time graveyard sexton, a keeper of the town clock (who also owned a jewelry store), and a keeper of the powder magazine (explosives were used to fight fires).

Periodic complaints in the antebellum press cited neglected streets and alleys, decaying bridges, and other public needs. In 1858 the *North Carolinian* took note that a railroad would soon link Fayetteville to the Chatham County coalfields, urged a movement to "paint up the town," and specifically called for repairs to the Market House.

Culture

Antebellum cultural pursuits included a full range of typical activities. The so-called "first poem published in North Carolina" was printed by the Fayetteville printshop of Sibley & Howard in 1790 and was appropriately titled "The Monitor, Or A Poem of Dancing Addressed to the Ladies and Gentlemen of the Fayetteville Assembly." (The Fayetteville Assembly was a dancing club.) Dancing was especially popular in town society. A grand affair in "the assembly room of the Lafayette Hotel" in 1825, hosted by several leading businessmen, was announced by an elaborate printed program. Dancing masters regularly advertised for customers. Dramatic presentations were held in the new State House in the 1790s, and a Thalian Society was chartered in 1814 to promote the dramatic arts.

In the 1790s a passion for horse racing gripped the county and indeed the entire state. Cumberland's leading men bred horses for racing, entered their steeds in the "Fayetteville Races," and frequently bet on their favorite contenders. The name of an early center of the sport is preserved in "Racepath Street," located near the Cape Fear River in Fayetteville. William Barry Grove, the young congressman from Fayetteville, was so enraged by the theft of a blooded animal in 1792 that he successfully rode down the thief, "almost to the frontiers of Georgia."

For the masses, there were popular attractions such as cockfighting; billiards; visits by street performers with exotic animals, especially monkeys; Fourth of July festivities; and the free barbecue and liquor of election days and militia musters. There was a Masonic lodge in Fayetteville known as the "Union Lodge" by 1784; it was supplanted in 1788 by the "Phenix" lodge.

By 1793 the town's Masons had obtained a site for a lodge hall, which was soon erected. This structure was enlarged in the early nineteenth century but was replaced in 1858 by a completely new facility that remains in use at the present time.

Education

The earliest antebellum educational projects in Cumberland were subscription "academies" or "seminaries" financed by patrons and tuition. Clergymen customarily were the founder-teachers of such schools. In them, young male and female scholars from families of the gentry studied classical subjects and were taught the social graces. In the 1840s the state launched a notable program of establishing public schools. By 1860 this program supported dozens of one-room schools in which even the children of laborers and small farmers received instruction for a few weeks each year from young teachers, male and female. There were also many specialized one-teacher schools offering instruction in dance, music, military training, and even fencing.

The principal early school in Cumberland County was Fayetteville Academy, begun as early as 1791 by the Reverend David Ker (1758-1805), a Dublin-trained Presbyterian clergyman who subsequently removed to Chapel Hill, where he became the first teacher at the University of North Carolina and for a brief time served as acting head of the institution. In 1798 eight leading citizens appealed for the establishment of a "well-regulated public seminary." The legislature responded by formally chartering Fayetteville Academy in 1799. For several years the commodious hall of Fayetteville's Masonic lodge was used for classes. In 1800 130 scholars—boys and girls—received instruction from the teachers, a Mr. Meroney and a Miss Taylor. Presbyterian ministers customarily doubled as teachers. A quarter-century later, in 1825, the academy was a familiar institution. A three-story structure "with a double portico in front . . . surmounted with a beautiful belfry," the academy stood on Green Street near St. John's Episcopal Church. The academy, which attracted students from surrounding communities and from South Carolina, was destroyed by fire in 1831.

Methodists established the Fayetteville School Association in 1814, seeking $25,000 for a building. Ravenscroft School was started by Episcopalians in 1831. Baptists had schools associated with churches, the "United Baptist Association" being chartered in

1855. Similar schools were chartered in small planter communities—Flea Hill Academy in 1831 and Silver Run Academy in 1855.

In 1833 another Fayetteville facility, the Donaldson Academy and Labor School, also sponsored by the Presbyterians, opened in imposing buildings on the brow of Haymount on a site that would be identified with education for 135 years. With many changes and financial difficulties, this institution continued to exist through the Civil War, and its old buildings were used by postwar public schools.

The school was named for Robert Donaldson (1800-1872), a principal benefactor who, although he left Fayetteville as a young man, is as much identified with the history of his hometown as with the broader history of American architecture and design. Born in a house overlooking the Newberry mill site, Donaldson was the son of a leading merchant and an 1818 graduate of the University of North Carolina in a class that included James K. Polk. He became rich when the death of a British uncle made him beneficiary of a considerable estate. For his hometown, Donaldson financed an elegant hotel on Hay Street known as the Lafayette, which was completed just in time for the visit of the marquis

The original Lafayette Hotel was erected on Hay Street in Fayetteville in 1825. It was named in honor of the marquis de Lafayette, who visited the town while on a tour of the United States during that year. The engraving of the hotel appears as a decorative vignette on the face of John MacRae's 1825 map of Fayetteville. Photograph from the files of the Division of Archives and History.

himself in March, 1825. The following year Donaldson left for New York. For forty years he was an important patron of American architecture and design. As such, Donaldson was associated with important state projects, including the State Capitol and structures at Chapel Hill.

The school bearing Donaldson's name was described in 1840 as being situated on a twenty-acre site "with a large two-story building, with wings," and "tolerable philosophical and chemical apparatus." There were also "two good two story dwelling houses, outhouses, and several small buildings used as dormitories." The main building included a cupola surmounted by a weather vane in the shape of "a female figure representing science," a device "made and executed by James Martine," a local artisan.

The most noted educator associated with this school was Simeon Colton (1785-1868), a Connecticut-born graduate of Yale and a Presbyterian minister, who was headmaster of the academy from its opening until 1846 and later served schools in Harnett and Randolph counties. A highly praised teacher, Colton was also a harsh disciplinarian and was frequently embroiled in controversy over church and school matters. In one letter, he complained about parents of his charges: "They want their children to do well, but to be indulged in every humor."

Another imposing building went up on Hay Street in 1854 for the Fayetteville Female Seminary, or "high school." It was the latest in a succession of educational institutions exclusively for girls. Efforts to educate Cumberland County's girls began as early as 1813 with the establishment of the "Female Orphan Asylum Society" and included a later "Female School of Industry." The two-story seminary building subsequently was used as a Civil War hospital, a hotel, a military academy, and a public school respectively.

Cumberland's participation in the antebellum public school effort began in 1839 when county voters approved a new state school law by a substantial margin. Under the law the county was entitled to receive an annual state allotment after it had established a local public-school facility. In 1844 the county court set the school-tax rate at 7 cents on the poll (a person legally eligible to vote) and 3 cents on each $100 worth of property owned. The tax produced a few hundred dollars annually and qualified the county to receive appropriations from the state school fund. By 1851 three-man committees had been named for seventy-three school districts in the county. Chairman Edward Lee

Winslow of the county committee estimated that 4,300 white children were eligible for schooling. In 1851 the county received $3,012 from the state school fund. In 1857 it received $2,126, the largest allocation for any county in North Carolina. Poor economic conditions reduced the annual appropriation to $1,300 on the eve of the Civil War, during which most efforts to improve the state's public schools were abandoned.

Teachers often were former pupils in the schools in which they conducted classes. Miss Sarah McFadyn was rated as the county's most qualified teacher in 1858. In the 1860 census for Cumberland approximately twenty-five people, about equally divided between male and female, are listed as schoolteachers.

The county's efforts in the field of public education were applied almost exclusively to white children. After 1830 it was illegal to teach a slave to read or write. But at least a few black children obtained training. By the 1850s ministers and volunteers in Presbyterian, Episcopal, Methodist, and Baptist churches in Fayetteville were teaching some youngsters of free-black families and a few slaves a basic curriculum created especially for them. Individual blacks often learned basics while serving as apprentices, artisans, or house servants.

Black History

Black people, slave and free, provided the basic work force of the county and town in the years between the Revolution and the Civil War. Their history is not one of famous individuals or events. But as the record is gleaned, it is clear that theirs was a richly varied existence, even under the burdens of slavery and restrictive laws.

Slaves. Black people in bondage comprised one fourth to two fifths of the county's population between 1790 and 1860. Several hundred slaves were owned as single individuals, either as workers on small farms or as house servants. The average slaveholder in Cumberland owned two families of slaves during the period. A handful of slave owners (who totaled 720 in 1840 and 809 in 1860) had as many as a dozen or more. In 1830, 39 percent of rural householders owned at least one slave. Three percent owned more than twenty. In that year the largest slaveholders were planter families. William Lord owned 89. The Eliot family of Ellerslie plantation on the Lower Little River and neighboring plantations owned 154, and the Evans family, who dwelt nearby, owned 124.

While the vast majority of slaves were farmhands, others—especially in town—were construction and blacksmith artisans, barbers, servants, riverboat hands, boat pilots, draymen, washerwomen, and wagoners. Newspapers were sprinkled with advertisements listing such people, either for rent or sale or sought as runaways. In 1816 Rose, "wellknown in this place, an excellent cook, washer, and ironer," was advertised for sale. Another whose name appeared frequently between 1801 and 1816 as a runaway was "Burklow's Peter," a carpenter "of much ingenuity" who could "read and write tolerably well." There were unnamed artisans such as the carpenters, coopers, and boatmen listed for rent by Robert Donaldson in 1823. John Cameron's estate sale two years later offered thirty slaves, including two "excellent tanners" as well as "two smiths, carpenters, and other mechanics." Other sales listed "a first rate waggoner, and two blacksmiths." Court records listed twenty slaves apprenticed for various trades during the antebellum period.

It is probable that black men helped to erect many of the principal buildings and other construction projects undertaken during the period, among them the State House and its successor the Market House, canals, railroads, and waterworks. In 1816 William Lumsden advertised for "colored boys" age twelve or thirteen to be apprenticed for bricklaying and plastering. Slave wagoners and draymen were so numerous around the Market House and mills that an ordinance required them to wear an identifying badge and their owners to pay a fee.

Surely one of Fayetteville's most noted antebellum citizens was midwife "Nurse Hannah" Mallet, who for seventy-five years had been the "property [nominally] of the Mallet family." When she died at the age of 102 in 1857, her obituary was as conspicuous as those for white civic and political leaders who died that year. She was "a pious member of the Episcopal church," and her funeral at St. John's was "attended by a large concourse of colored and a number of whites."

Freedom. A few slaves gained the status of freemen. Nelson Henderson, twenty-two-year-old slave barber, was freed in 1813. He was a longtime musician for militia units and upon his death in 1874 was buried "with full military honors." In 1814 Thomas Grymes freed Maria, a female slave and servant of Elizabeth Winslow, granting "full and perfect liberty from all slavery and bondage" and naming her Maria Grymes. In his 1823 will William Russell, a leading founder of the town of Cross Creek, ordered his slaves liberated and given money for travel to free states. In 1833 Joseph Hostler and Horace Henderson, slave barbers, were emancipated by the legislature, and Lovey Ann Henderson, Horace's wife, was freed upon the payment of $870 to her owner. In 1842 James Revels, a free black, sought in his will to have his wife, Jenet, freed, and he prayed that "my worthy friends" would apply to the legislature for her emancipation. As late as 1858 Jane Beze Perry, widow of a prominent merchant, sought to free the family slaves by having some males sent to free states, allowing others to choose their own new masters, and requesting emancipation for a house servant, Caroline, age forty-one, and her five children, including fourteen-year-old Benjie, who was willed his master's gold watch.

Insurrections, Punishments, Sales. Alarms concerning slave revolts punctuated the antebellum years. Such actual events as the successful revolution by slaves in the Caribbean in the 1790s and the Nat Turner Rebellion in Southampton County, Virginia, in 1831 triggered specific reactions. The former prompted establishment of a small arsenal of federal arms in Fayetteville. In the hysterical aftermath of the latter, charges of making insurrection were brought against six Cumberland slaves. Two of the six— named Dave and Bristow—were convicted and ordered to be hanged.

In a period during which criminal law was harsh, punishment for slaves was especially brutal. In 1795 "the Negro Morris," charged with murder and convicted of manslaughter, was tied to a cask and given fifty lashes on his bare back, "well laid on at the courthouse." He was then "taken to the top of the hill," branded on both cheeks with the letter *M*, and given fifty more lashes.

Being chattels, slaves were sold like other property, especially when estates were being settled or when white slave owners decided to leave the county. In the 1790s an average of about three such sales took place each month. In the 1830s traveling slave buyers occasionally advertised in Fayetteville newspapers, usually seeking boys or young men. In one instance, a construction company that had just completed a railroad in South Carolina advertised to sell the entire crew of more than thirty workers, including female cooks and seamstresses.

Runaways. The most audacious black people were those who attempted to escape from slavery by becoming runaways. Advertisements offering rewards for the capture and return of these people to their owners provide a rich sampling of what might be called a census of the intrepid. Some descriptions of runaways from newspaper advertisements published in the 1830s include:

Eli Terry, 16. Light color. Five-foot high. Wearing a drab coat, old fur hat and a cotton handkerchief for a cravat, a blue-striped waistcoat, a pair of copper-colored breeches, patched at the knees. Scar on inner left foot, an axe cut. He was last seen in company of a wagoneer from the back country. Ranaway from plantation of David Terry.

Lucy Ann Nelson, 15, apprentice girl of color, is a runaway from Thomas Moore of Beaver Crk.

John Leman, a blacksmith, and Jerry and Ben, laborers, were working on canal of the Cape Fear Navigation Company. Ranaway.

David, a spunky fellow. Ranaway from Fayetteville.

Free Blacks. Free blacks formed a small but significant group. Many of the county's most notable black families descended from these antebellum ancestors. The black population of Fayetteville as enumerated in the first census of 1790 totaled 32 free black heads of household and 522 slaves. In 1800 there were 67 free black heads of household and 626 slaves in the town. An additional 52 free blacks and 1,097 slaves resided within Cumberland County but outside of Fayetteville. The number of "free persons of color" ranged as high as 757 in 1840; this number was about equally divided between the town and rural areas of the county. Free blacks thus constituted from 5 to 10 percent of the town population and much less in the rural countryside.

Free blacks were permitted to vote prior to 1835. In 1810, as noted earlier, a disputed election for borough representative in the legislature turned in part on charges of undue influence by free black Isaac Hammond, a Revolutionary War veteran and militia musician, and the voting credentials of Thomas Sampson, "a mulatto Fellow," were questioned.

Constraints on free blacks and slaves increased unceasingly. A law enacted in 1785 required free blacks in Fayetteville to wear distinctive shoulder badges with the legend "FREE" and established restrictions on their mobility, choice of occupation, and relationship with slaves. A 1794 law "for the better regulation of Fayetteville" elaborated on these restrictions. A "patrol act" in 1805 granted new authority to regulate the movement of free blacks. In 1826 an ordinance regulating both slave and free black conduct decreed that "no slave or free negro shall smoke a pipe or seegar in any street, lane, or alley, or open place in Fayetteville, or walk with a cane or club, or other stick (except such as are infirm or blind), or carry about him any weapon." The act also forbade "whooping or hallooing," as well as "any indecent or impudent conduct." Fines were levied against free black offenders. Slaves were whipped. White tavern owners who remained open for business after 9:00 P.M. "to serve slaves" could lose their licenses.

Among Fayetteville's notable free blacks were Africa Parker, a drayman-artisan with the mercantile firm of Hogg & Adam in 1799; Isaac, a chair maker and carpenter in 1801; John Patterson, a carpenter-builder who emigrated to Ohio; Isaac Hammond and Nelson Henderson, barbers; and, most important, Matthew Leary (1802-1880). Leary, born in Sampson County, was operating a saddle and harness shop at the corner of Person and Dick streets in Fayetteville by the 1820s. Many young black men, slave and free, worked in the shop. Several, including two of Leary's sons, emigrated to Ohio in the 1850s and became leaders in that state's notable community of former southern free blacks. Leary's oldest son, Lewis Sheridan Leary, was an early martyr for black freedom. He was killed at Harpers Ferry, Virginia, in 1859 as a member of John Brown's raiding party. Matthew Leary was a man of considerable substance. In 1857, apparently contemplating leaving North Carolina, he advertised for sale a 500-acre farm, his home and shop, ten shares of stock in the Cape Fear Bank, and twelve shares of stock in a plank road company. During the post-Civil War period Leary served as a leader among free blacks and as a public official.

Some free blacks did manage to leave the county. The most noteworthy emigrants left Fayetteville in 1856, joining a wagon train to Ohio. Among them was the grandmother of Langston Hughes, a black poet of the twentieth century, and the parents of pioneering black novelist Charles Waddell Chesnutt.

Women

While most women of the antebellum period remained at home, in a cotton factory, or perhaps in a classroom, some operated businesses, especially taverns and inns or millinery shops. Ellen Duffy maintained a "millinery establishment" in the 1790s, and a Mrs. Crawford opened "a house for the entertainment of gentleman travelers" (a tavern) in Fayetteville in 1800. Some fifty years later Mrs. E. Watson opened a millinery shop "at a new stand on Green Street." Seven women listed themselves as milliners in the 1860 census.

Widows of noted tavern keepers operated such establishments as "Mrs. [Lewis] Barge's" and "Mrs. [George] Fletcher's" (1751-1824). In the 1850s Ann Brown was the proprietor of the Fayetteville Hotel, "the largest and handsomest in North Carolina." Another important female role was in health care. "Mrs. [Mary] Hybart, a midwife," arrived in Fayetteville from England in 1807. (Her son, Thomas, became an important local lawyer, editor, and politician in the 1830s.) In Fayetteville, especially, women were also involved in civic and religious affairs to some extent, spurring men to organize library societies, educational societies, and efforts to aid orphans.

Violence

Violence—criminal, political, and domestic—was common in antebellum life. During much of the period, dueling was an accepted alternative in public controversy. In 1800 Colonel Thomas Davis and a "Dr. Jordan" faced off near Fayetteville. They "took two fire, in the second both received a wound nearly in the same place in the groin." The local newspaper account concluded: "Happy to hear they are on the recovery." It was not all so genteel. The political strife of the period led to tragedy on the dueling grounds. Archibald McDiarmid, a noted political figure from rural 71st Township and four-time state senator, was killed in a political duel with James Atkins in 1846.

Not all violence was politically motivated. In 1790 the state, citing "frequent and atrocious robberies," offered a reward for the capture of Seth Colter and John Abbot, "leaders of a gang of villains now infesting the neighborhood of Fayetteville." In 1801 William Travers was "kicked to death" by Sheriff Stephen Gilmore in an altercation related to a card game that took place in the Fayetteville store of Robert Donaldson. The most celebrated of all violent crimes occurring in Cumberland County was the arsenic poisoning of Alexander C. Simpson in November, 1849. The victim's wife, Ann K. Simpson, was tried for murder a year later in Fayetteville. Noted local lawyers represented each side, with former judge Robert Strange, the Winslows, and Duncan MacRae achieving victory when a jury found Mrs. Simpson not guilty. The trial proceedings, juicy with testimony about illicit love and the alleged influence of Polly Rising, a fortune-teller, were widely printed. An edition of 750 copies sold out overnight in Fayetteville.

Religion

Cumberland's colonial religious heritage—mainly Presbyterian, Quaker, and Baptist—shared in the gradual quickening of religious interest and denominational zeal in the antebellum years. Presbyterian congregations at Bluff, Barbecue, and Longstreet were joined in 1800 by new churches in Fayetteville and on the lands of Colin McPherson (1759-1834) a few miles west. By the 1790s, permanent clergymen were settling in Fayetteville; the town congregation erected a handsome, steepled church in 1815. It looked across to St. John's Episcopal Church, organized in 1817. These buildings were destroyed by fire in 1831 and were replaced by substantial brick structures.

Old Bluff Presbyterian Church is the oldest organized Presbyterian congregation in present Cumberland County, having been formed in 1758. This structure, erected in the mid-1850s, is the fourth meetinghouse to serve the congregation. It is among the finest temple-form Greek Revival church buildings in the upper Cape Fear region. A new Bluff Presbyterian Church in Wade supplanted Old Bluff in 1908, but the latter is maintained and used as the site of an annual homecoming. Photograph from the files of the Division of Archives and History; information supplied by Survey and Planning Branch, State Historic Preservation Office.

For much of the town's history a large proportion of its leading citizens were members of one or the other of these congregations. Two Episcopal rectors served for a total of fifty-seven years: Jarvis P. Buxton from 1831 to 1851 and Joseph Caldwell Huske from 1851 until his death in 1888. Bishop Francis Asbury, the traveling father of American Methodism, was in Cross Creek as early as 1783. One of Asbury's associates preached in the new State House during a 1788 visit.

Cumberland's most famous Methodist churchman was Henry Evans, a free black cobbler-preacher, who arrived in Fayetteville in the last years of the eighteenth century and was soon preaching to a large, racially mixed audience at his little slab chapel beside Cross Creek. At his death in 1810 Evans had firmly established Methodism in the village. There was a Sunday school by 1819, and a wood-frame sanctuary was erected on Old Street in 1834. Evangelical Methodism flamed in rural areas. An 1825 camp meeting eight miles from Fayetteville reportedly drew a crowd of 6,000 people. Congregations formed in such rural districts as Flea Hill (Salem Church) and 71st Township (Campground Church).

Baptists, with colonial congregations at Cape Fear and Beaver Dam, did not organize in Fayetteville until 1837, but the congregation quickly became one of the largest in town. Its frame church on the corner of Old and Union (now Anderson) streets looked across Eccles Pond to the older and more elegant Presbyterian and Episcopal churches. James McDaniel, its first pastor (1837-1844 and 1852-1869), born in rural Cumberland, was for nineteen years president of the State Baptist Convention and a longtime trustee of Wake Forest College, where he was a student in 1837-1838. A rural Baptist leader was Elder William Thames (1760-1813), a native son of the congregation at Cape Fear.

Unusual for the rural South, Fayetteville had a small but well-to-do Roman Catholic church, organized in 1829 through the influence of Irish immigrant John Kelly, a leading merchant-planter, and the Dillon Jordans, father and son. The senior Jordan (1777-1837), a native of County Mayo, Ireland, was a noted tavern keeper. The junior was a well-known lawyer-politician. The Roman Catholic congregation's handsome frame chapel, erected in 1829 on Bow Street, was rebuilt after an 1831 fire and continued to serve as a place of worship for 103 years.

The 1850 census enumerated 12 Baptist, 8 Methodist, 5 Presbyterian, 5 Episcopal, and 5 Roman Catholic churches in Cumberland County. In these churches, white parishioners were joined by a scattering of free blacks and slave members. In the 1850s some blacks were able to organize their own congregations. The "Methodist Episcopal Church for the Colored Persons of Fayetteville," a congregation of free blacks, repurchased the site of the old Evans chapel on Cross Creek in 1854. Flea Hill African Methodist Zion Church, east of the Cape Fear, dates from 1855.

The influence of evangelical religion was expressed not only in church growth but also in temperance societies, Sunday schools, fund-raising events for the poor, and efforts to improve conditions for widows, orphans, or runaway girls. The "Female School of Industry," chartered in 1831, was one such effort.

Fires

The first of the spectacular fires in Fayetteville's history began on a warm autumn night, October 23, 1792, when a young slave girl's bedtime candle set off a blaze in the loft of Colonel Lee Dekeyser's tavern just up the west side of Green Street from the four-year-old State House. Before the blaze ran its course, more than thirty structures had been destroyed. The corpse of William Crawford, "a laboring man," was discovered in the ruins of the tavern's public room. The fire was a heavy blow to the village of 300 families. But there was praise for the Fayetteville Fire Company, which had been chartered in 1791. A boon for historians was a full, vivid account of the tragedy in the *Fayetteville Gazette* of October 30, an early example of reportorial journalism. In 1794 another fire, almost in the same spot, destroyed several structures, notably the brand-new home and dependencies of Dr. John Silbey, a newspaper publisher who recently had been appointed Fayetteville's postmaster.

The most famous conflagration came thirty-seven years later on May 29, 1831, when "About 15 minutes before 12 o'clock A.M. on Sunday" the roof of the kitchen of a building very near the same spot was seen to be burning. Within hours, much of the town was destroyed. No deaths or injuries were reported, but ninety-eight individuals, firms, or estates suffered loss of property. Among the structures destroyed were the Town House; Episcopal, Presbyterian, and Roman Catholic churches; the Bank of Cape Fear; the Fayetteville Academy; and the Lafayette and Mansion hotels. The fire attracted national attention. Nearly $100,000 in relief donations came from churches, businesses, and individuals throughout the United States. A Boston fire company donated a handsome pumping engine that became the prize equipment of the Phoenix Fire Company, chartered in 1834. Rebuilding was prompt. On May 30, 1832, the *Fayetteville Journal* reported that 166 houses had been rebuilt and that twenty others were under construction. New church buildings were being used. "A Town House with a market underneath" stood on the site of the old facility. It was soon referred to almost exclusively as the "Market House."

On June 6, 1845, a fire began in a warehouse on the north side of Hay Street, 300 yards from the Market House. The conflagration destroyed fifty-four buildings, about one third of those in Fayetteville. Tempers flared in the wake of this blaze. Arson was suspected. A $250 reward was offered for "the person who fired the town." A newspaper correspondent criticized the quality of Fayetteville's fire companies, charging that they were "composed of men seeking to dodge military service" and accusing them of "rescuing goods instead of fighting fire." The writer proposed that "they should have colored men in the companies," citing the selfless performance of propertyless slaves and free blacks who fought the fire of 1831. By 1848 a total of forty-eight black men were said to comprise two engine companies and a hook-and-ladder company.

Barely a year after the 1845 blaze, another fire destroyed twenty-five or thirty buildings on Green and Person streets in Fayetteville. Within a year, new structures, built mostly of brick, had replaced the destroyed edifices.

Military Affairs

Military affairs during the period from the Revolution to the Civil War were a mixture of the serious and not-so-serious. There was the seriousness of actual war—against Great Britain, 1812-1814, and against Mexico, 1846-1848—as well as occasional alarms over actual or suspected problems arising from "slave insurrections," such as those which occurred in Haiti, 1791-1804, and in northeastern North Carolina in 1831. During these times, local militia units shouldered arms in earnest.

There were also the not-so-serious occasions during which volunteer militia companies donned uniforms and performed at musters, Fourth of July festivities, and special events such as the visit by the marquis de Lafayette in 1825. Militia companies included the Fayetteville Independent Light Infantry, which was established in 1793 when war with England threatened (or possibly in response to the slave uprisings in Haiti). Many village leaders were members of the antebellum Independent Light Infantry, which remains in existence at the present time. The Partisan Light Dragoons of Fayetteville paraded in tribute to the recently deceased George Washington in 1800. By 1811 the county militia was mustered in two distinct battalions of several companies each. By the time of Lafayette's 1825 visit, three additional militia units—the Lafayette Light Infantry, the Fayetteville Corps of Artillery, and the Fayetteville Light Horse—had been organized.

During the War of 1812 three companies of citizen soldiers were gleaned from Cumberland's militia units, but these units did not actually take part in battle. The Fayetteville Independent Light Infantry marched briefly to Wilmington in the summer of 1813, when a British invasion was feared. A fourth company of "detached" militia was called up late in 1814 and apparently marched to Wilmington with other companies from the Cape Fear valley. A total of 201 men were listed as members of one company or another.

As the Mexican War approached, a company known as the Fayetteville Riflemen was chartered with William H. Bayne (d. 1851), fiery Democratic newspaper editor, as captain. By then, militia service was voluntary, and the companies were as much social and political as military organizations. No county units actually served in Mexico, and Bayne's volunteer voted not to participate in such service. Cumberland did, however, provide the men who comprised Company I of the North Carolina Regiment of Volunteers.

Arsenals

A unique aspect of Cumberland County in antebellum military affairs was the fact that the county was home to three arsenals during the period. A small "federal arsenal" was established in Fayetteville, perhaps as early as 1790. When the War of 1812 began, this facility was said to contain "150 guns, canteens, tents, knapsacks, and a small quantity of powder." State officials had difficulty securing the munitions until late in the war, when there were threats of a British invasion of the coast. In 1820 the town was designated as the site for a state arsenal. An appropriation in the amount of $750 from the legislature financed a small brick building. In it, small arms and two field pieces of a local volunteer unit known as the Flying Corps of Artillery were kept under lock and key. An 1825 map of Fayetteville locates the arsenal at the northeast corner of Lamon and Ramsey streets. In 1822 arms from Edenton and New Bern were ordered stored there. In 1836-1837 the legislature ordered "the public arms at Fayetteville and Raleigh to be repaired" and enumerated 816 muskets in the Fayetteville inventory.

By far the most significant military installation in antebellum North Carolina—other than the state's coastal forts—was the United States Arsenal, built on the Haymount eminence beginning in 1838. One of four such facilities authorized by Congress in 1836, it was pushed to completion over a decade of on-again, off-again appropriations. Its designer, Scottish-born William Bell (1783-1865), had worked on government buildings in Washington, as well as another arsenal in Charleston, South Carolina. He arrived in Fayetteville in 1838 to supervise construction and never left, becoming a noted citizen of the community. So did Captain A. J. Bradford (d. 1863), a longtime commander of the arsenal and zealous lobbyist for funds when construction languished, who lowered the Stars and Stripes when Confederates seized the

The United States Arsenal was constructed in Fayetteville beginning in 1838. By the 1850s the forty-acre complex included a main building, octagonal corner towers, officers' quarters, barracks, shops, and well-tended grounds. The arsenal played an important role in the Civil War and in 1865 fell into the hands of an invading force of Union soldiers, resulting in the destruction by fire of most of its component structures. Engraving from *Harper's Weekly*, IX (April 1, 1865), 197.

arsenal in April, 1861. By the 1850s, the forty-acre complex included a handsome brick-and-stone main building, octagonal corner towers, officers' quarters, barracks, shops, and well-tended grounds. It was regarded as a local attraction by proud townspeople and visitors alike, and it played an important role in the Civil War.

Medicine

Cumberland County was a center of antebellum medical practice, as it had been since the 1760s, when Joseph Howard, "doctor of physic," and Thomas McDaniel Reed, "surgeon," were active in the village of Cross Creek. Dr. Ben Robinson, mentioned earlier, practiced for more than a half-century after 1805. His son, B. W. Robinson (1811-1885), matched his record. J. A. MacRae was a founding member of the North Carolina Medical Society. A county society with a dozen members was founded in 1853. Dr. Ben Robinson's account book, preserved at Duke University, details a typical medical practice of the period. It lists a round of daily house calls punctuated by occasional attendance at a birth. Robinson charged $15.00 for his services in connection with the latter.

Periodic alarms over threatened epidemics of yellow fever or cholera mobilized the medical community. In 1832 four physicians designated as the "Board of Health" for Fayetteville issued a broadside detailing sanitary measures necessary to fight "Asiatic or Spasmodic Cholera." Despite such measures and in spite of the relative abundance of medical practitioners, most people in antebellum Cumberland County went through life—and death— with only minimal medical attention or none at all. Slaves and whites in rural areas generally treated their own illnesses and injuries as best they could.

The annual report of interments in Fayetteville's town cemetery for the year 1857 provides a general picture of average life expectancy during the period. Of 102 people who died that year, 16 were under five years of age, 29 were under thirty, another 27 were between the ages of thirty and fifty, and the remaining 30 were above fifty, including one who died at the age of 102.

Agriculture

Farming was basic to the Cumberland economy in the antebellum period. "Planter" and "farmer" were the most prevalent occupational listings. Typical North Carolina crops, first tobacco and then cotton, predominated. Grain and cattle, staples of the colonial period, remained more important in Cumberland than generally in the state.

Tobacco. Tobacco enjoyed a vigorous but relatively brief heyday as a major crop in the last years of the colonial period and the first decades of the new republic. Colonial Campbellton had its official tobacco warehouse in 1770. The post of tobacco inspector was a popular one, with a yearly stipend of £40 in 1774. Some planters specialized in the complex planting and curing process. John Gray was apprenticed to William Thompson in 1779 to "learn the trade of tobacconist."

The production of tobacco was encouraged as a means of paying the state's Revolutionary War debts. Leading men were growers, inspectors, and warehousemen. By 1792 three firms had warehouses in Fayetteville capable of storing 6,000 hogsheads. There was also a "tobacco factory" near the Cape Fear River; it was an *L*-shaped structure with wings 50 feet long and 40 feet wide, and it was equipped "with screws" (presses used to pack tobacco into hogsheads) and "convenient store rooms."

A quarter-century later, in 1816, tobacco "boated from Fayetteville" on the Cape Fear totaled 2,337 hogsheads with a total value of $400,000. But even then, cotton had become more important. By 1824 the tobacco trade was 1,500 hogsheads; a year later only 763 hogsheads and 300 kegs of the leaf were shipped, and the riverside factory was for sale. In 1834 volume was down to 133 hogsheads. Tobacco was not even mentioned in the agricultural census of 1840.

Cotton. The invention of the cotton gin and subsequent demand made cotton Cumberland's leading money crop after 1800, a distinction it would hold for more than a century. The economy rose and fell with the price of cotton. In 1816 cotton trade on the Cape Fear amounted to 8,282 bales, with a total value of $621,900. The Panic of 1819 sent prices plunging from 30 cents a pound to less than 15 cents. The Panic of 1837 drove the price to a pre-Civil War low of 9 cents. "Everybody is failing," a correspondent reported. For another twenty years the price of cotton fluctuated at levels below 20 cents a pound, averaging 12 cents on the eve of the Civil War.

It is difficult to ascertain just how much cotton was grown in Cumberland. The annual river trade amounted to as much as 15,000 bales (at approximately 300 pounds each) in the 1820s. But in 1840 the incomplete farm census listed only one-eighth that much actually produced in the county. Undoubtedly a large portion of the river traffic was from other counties.

Grain and Cattle. Grain and cattle, the basis of colonial agriculture, lingered into the nineteenth century. In 1840 the 19,000 head of cattle and 21,400 sheep listed by Cumberland farmers represented herds twice as large as the North Carolina per capita average. There were also nearly 40,000 hogs in Cumberland in 1840. A harvest of 404,000 bushels of corn sustained the herds.

Public Works

A zeal for "internal improvements" characterized the antebellum years. There were some notable successes—and many disappointments—among the plentiful schemes for roads, railroads, canals, and improvements to navigation.

Clearly a success was the Clarendon Bridge, built across the Cape Fear River at Fayetteville in 1819. The rugged wooden structure, a prototype of the "New England covered bridge," was designed by Ithiel Town (1784-1844), who obtained a patent in 1820 for his "Town truss" design for building sturdy, relatively low-cost bridging. Town also designed the North Carolina State Capitol and was considered the nation's leading architectural designer of the antebellum period. He resided in Fayetteville for several years as bridge superintendent, collecting tolls to finance its construction. Another successful public works project was the Fayetteville Water Works, chartered in 1819 and built by 1824, which employed wooden pipes to collect spring water on Haymount and distribute it to street reservoirs.

Not so successful was the Fayetteville Canal Company (1790), chartered to make Cross Creek navigable into the center of town; the Cape-Fear Company (1792), organized to make the river navigable from the confluence of the Haw and Deep rivers; and the "Stone Bridge lottery" (1806), which sought to raise $2,400 to span Cross Creek with a more substantial bridge.

The Cape Fear Navigation Company, chartered in 1791 to make the river a commercial artery, was a pet scheme of

Archibald Debow Murphey, North Carolina's leading proponent of state-financed internal improvements. When Murphey's scheme failed to attract backers, Murphey was harsh on Cumberland. He wrote from Fayetteville in 1819: "Nothing . . . vexes me more the perverse and contrary Spirit, which actuates the People of this place in all things relating to our Company's Proceedings."

River Transportation

The centrality of the Cape Fear River as an artery of transportation and trade affords a colorful and endlessly detailed story of antebellum life. There were numerous (and often unsuccessful) schemes to tame the river, to make it more dependable (it often ran near-dry in summer), and to capitalize on its potential. Fayetteville's link to the river was symbolized by the town's 1835 official seal, which depicts a steamboat as an emblem.

The antebellum period opened with the chartering of the Cape Fear Navigation Company by merchant-developers from Fayetteville and Wilmington. The company immediately advertised for construction of typical bateauxlike river vessels. It wanted two boats 48 feet long and 10 feet wide, with a 10-foot rake and two 80 feet long and 6 feet wide, with a 6-foot rake. The boats' sides were to be 2 feet high, with 2-inch planking. Such shallow-draft boats were pulled upriver by rowing crews in smaller boats and "poled" downriver. A boat advertised for sale in 1807 was capable, according to its owner, of carrying "1700 burthen [pounds] of salt or 20 hogsheds."

These boats were joined in 1818 by the first steamer. The *Henrietta* was built at the plantation of James Seawell a mile above Fayetteville and named for his daughter. Thereafter, the departures, arrivals, and cargoes of this boat and others were major news items in local newspapers. Low water often played havoc with the vessel's schedule, but it was proudly noted that during a rare time of optimum water conditions the *Henrietta* was capable of a return trip upriver from Wilmington in the impressive time of twenty-one hours. More than a dozen other small side-wheelers and stern-wheelers were on the river before 1860. Some were built in Fayetteville, among them the steamer *John Dawson*, named for its Wilmington owner and built by W. J. Russell in 1857. The *Dawson*, typical of the class, was described as having been 86 feet long and 17 feet wide. It drew 13 inches of water and had a stern wheel. Such boats could be hailed at riverside landings

STEAM  BOATS

Henrietta & North Carolina.

RATES OF FREIGHT, INCLUDING TOLL.

DOWN.

Cotton	bale	\$0 50	Bacon, Tallow, &c.	hhd.	\$1
Tobacco	hhd.	2	Lard, Oil, and Spirits	bbl.	40
Ditto, manufactured	keg	25	Do. and Butter	firkin	25
Flour	bbl.	30	Bacon, unpacked	ton	3
Flaxseed, Wheat, &c.	tierce	60	Corn, Wheat, and Oats	bushel	10
Feathers	bag	30	Boxes, Bales, Trunks, &c.	cu. foot	10

UP.

Salt, coarse, 10 cts.: Sound, 9 cts.: fine, 8 cts.	bushel		Cotton Bagging	piece	40
Sugar, 750 to 1250 lbs.	hhd.	\$2 25	Spades and Shovels	bundle	25
Do. 1250 to 1750 lbs.	hhd.	3 25	Frying Pans	bundle	40
Do. over 1750 lbs.	hhd.	4	Anvils	each	25
Molasses, Spirits, and Coffee	hhd.	2 25	Smiths' Vices	each	25
Do. do. and Oil	bbl.	75	Sheet Iron, bundle	112 lbs.	40
Wine	qr. cask	90	Fire Fenders	each	25
Do. and Spirits	pipe	3 00	Brass Andirons	pair	25
Rice, Coffee, and Sugar	tierce	1 60	Tin plate	box	25
Apples and Potatoes, (small 40 cts.) common			Copper, (in sheets, loose)	ton	5
size	bbl.	50	Do. in boxes	foot	20
Loaf and Brown Sugar	bbl.	60	Jugs, Jars, and Crocks	each	5
Coffee, Pepper, Pimento, and Ginger	bag	50	Wrapping paper	ream	8
Boxes, Trunks, Bales, Hhds. Tierces, Casks,			Band Boxes	nest	15
Hardware and Dry Goods	cu. foot	12½	Bottles, (loose)	each	1
Crockery, Glass, Tin ware, Jugs and Bottles,			Logwood	ton	4
packed	cu. foot	10	Hides	each	10
Paints, 28 lb.	keg	10	Hay	bale	1
Powder (loose)	keg	50	Mill Stones	each	5
Do. packed in boxes or casks	keg	37½	Grind Stones	ton	4
Shot and Lead (500 lbs.)	keg	1	Plaster Paris	ton	3
Bar Iron	ton	3 50	Lime	cask	75
Castings	ton	6	Setting Chairs	each	25
Nails, under 100 lbs. 25 cts.: 100 and not o-			Wheels and Shafts for Gig		2
ver 200 lbs.	keg	40	Jersey Wagons	each	4
Do. over 200 lbs.	keg	50	Ploughs	each	50

☞ Articles not enumerated to be charged in proportion to the above rates.

☞ *Prices of Lighterage.*—In low water, on the down freight, 25 per cent.: on up freight, from and below Elizabeth, 33 1-3 per cent., and above Elizabeth 15 per cent., will be added to the above rates.

☞ Produce for Wilmington will be received in the Steam Boat Warehouse at Fayetteville, free of Wharfage and Storage. Goods by the Steam Boats from Wilmington will (if required) be stored free, Salt and Lime excepted. Goods for Fayetteville will be received in the Steam Boat Warehouse, Wilmington, free of Wharfage and Storage. Produce from Fayetteville by the Steam Boats, may be stored in Wilmington free of Wharfage and Storage the first week, and half rates Storage afterwards. Subject, however, in all cases of Storage, to the risk of the owners, and not the Steam Boat Company.

☞ The Steam Boat Company hold themselves bound for the good condition of their Boats, the care, skill, and attention, of their officers and men; but in all cases, whether bills lading to that effect be taken or not, *the dangers of the river are excepted*, the greatest of which they consider unknown or unavoidable snags and logs.

WM. L. McNEILL, *Fayetteville,* ⎱ AGENTS.
HENRY R. SAVAGE, *Wilmington,* ⎰

Fayetteville, 7th August, 1825.

This broadside, issued in Fayetteville in August, 1825, provides a listing of commodities transported aboard the steamboats *Henrietta* and *North Carolina*, which regularly plied the Cape Fear River between Fayetteville and Wilmington. Broadside courtesy North Carolina Collection.

and plantations. One compiler listed more than forty such stops in Cumberland.

In the latter years of the antebellum period, the steamboat line of Thomas S. Lutterloh was the leading river enterprise based in Fayetteville. In 1858 a major tragedy occurred when fifteen people perished in the burning of the *Magnolia*, one of Lutterloh's vessels, near White Oak Landing in Bladen County. Among the victims were John M. Stedman, captain of the *Magnolia*, and "several black boys" who were members of the crew.

One of the rarities of antebellum river transportation was a sailing vessel under construction at Fayetteville in June, 1829, by "Captain Vandusen of Philadelphia." The *North Carolina Journal* reported that "the schooner of 100 tons" was "the first rigged vessel ever built on the Cape Fear River." The schooner was to be launched in August and to be sailed to Wilmington if the water were deep enough. There was no further mention of this project.

Railroads and Plank Roads

No place in North Carolina began earlier or worked harder than Fayetteville to become a railroad center. Subscription books for the Cape Fear & Yadkin Valley Railroad were opened in the town in 1832. Two years later experimental tracks were laid between the river landing and the Market House. The rudimentary railroad utilized horse-drawn cars to convey up to thirty passengers or four tons of freight. The wooden rails, which featured an unusually rounded center, proved unsatisfactory ("the friction is very great"), and within a few weeks two passengers were injured "in a careless accident on the railroad." Despite continuous effort, the railroad dream was not to be realized until just prior to the Civil War, when the Western Railroad Company completed track from Fayetteville to the Egypt Coal Mine (present Cumnock in Lee County).

Frustrated in the struggle for preeminence in the realm of railroad construction, Cumberland developers turned in the 1840s to the plank road, a mode of transportation then enjoying its heyday in Pennsylvania. At least six such lines were projected from Fayetteville in every direction. The most notable was the Western Plank Road, built between 1849 and 1854 to link the town with its old trading partner of Salem. The 129-mile-long road from the Market House to Salem was billed as the longest such artery ever constructed. The trip by stagecoach took eighteen hours, which contrasted quite remarkably with the three-day colonial-era journey along sandhill trading paths. Toll keepers in small houses located at intervals along the road collected revenues, which totaled $27,419 in 1854, the peak year. By the time of the Civil War the road was already in financial difficulty, and much of it simply disappeared during the conflict. The terminal segment of the road down Hay Street was covered over and largely forgotten. In 1982, however, engineers and archaeologists were amazed and delighted when a downtown resurfacing project uncovered virtually intact portions of the 130-year-old roadway.

Commerce

The commerce of the Cape Fear valley was centered in Fayetteville, which began as a trading settlement and remained so. The town's streets were lined with mercantile establishments and the shops of artisans. Its gristmills, sawmills, tanneries, and breweries converted products of the countryside into salable commodities. Blacksmiths, wheelwrights, coopers, and tinsmiths made the tools, vehicles, barrels, and stills needed for farming, boating, and manufacturing turpentine. Taverns and hotels served travelers and visitors. Banks and cotton brokers served financial needs.

An early post-Revolutionary description of commercial life was the entry for Fayetteville in a 1795 national gazetteer, which credited the town with three mills, two distilleries, and several tanneries. Newspapers of the period mentioned a dozen or so mercantile businesses, the largest being the store of the Hogg family firm, known in Fayetteville as Hogg & [Robert] Adam. Newspapers listed the products of the county as tobacco, wheat, flour, lumber, staves, and naval stores. Flatboats capable of carrying up to 150 barrels each plied the Cape Fear between Fayetteville and Wilmington.

In the 1820s there were gristmills, tanneries, a shoe "factory," a carriage manufactory, a flaxseed-oil mill, and the ever-present sawmills. In 1835 seventy-five mercantile businesses were listed in tax records, mostly in Fayetteville. The tax rate was based on the amount of "stock in trade" in each store. Eight of the seventy-five paid the top rate for an inventory of $15,000 or more. Forty paid the minimum rate for an inventory of less than $5,000. In 1852 ninety-nine store operators bought licenses, with twelve paying the maximum rate.

What did these merchants sell? Statistics concerning the river trade reveal the extent of mercantile activity. In 1825 Fayetteville merchants brought in 67,697 bushels of salt, 1,028 hogsheads of sugar and molasses, 7,888 barrels of spirits, 283 tons of iron, and 60,628 feet of "measurable merchandise" (cloth). In 1834 these "imports" included 2,284 hogsheads, 3,495 barrels, and 373 tierces (43-gallon casks) of merchandise; 349 tons of iron; 1,531 casks of limestone; and 80,399 bushels of salt.

Notable "merchant princes" who fashioned the town's early nineteenth-century economy are buried in Cross Creek Cemetery beneath handsome gravestones alluding to their contributions in the realm of commerce. They include Andrew Broadfoot (1765-1801), "native of Glasgow, a late merchant of this town"; Oliver Pearce (1765-1815), "merchant," a native of Rhode Island; Paris Jencks Tillinghast (1757-1822); Duncan McLeran (1760-1821) of Argyllshire, Scotland, and "for many years a respectable merchant of this place"; Robert Adam (1759-1801), a native of Grenock, Scotland, and "for many years a merchant in Fayetteville & Wilmington"; and Robert Halliday (1786-1828), a native of Galloway, Scotland, and "a merchant of this place." There were many others, including George McNeill, the Stedmans, Cochrans, Eccleses, Donaldsons, Haighs, Kyles, Fullers, Mallets, and Huskes. Some of these merchants, such as a "Mr. Martin, a retailer of whiskey and onions in one of the shops on Hay Street," were not so grand. There were unusual businesses such as that of Sebastian Staiert, a noted Episcopal layman, whose "shop for scents and perfumes" was an early nineteenth-century emporium. The "Jewish merchant" tradition began as early as 1818, when Jacob Levy & Co. opened a business on Hay Street.

Banking

Fayetteville was an antebellum banking center. A branch of the Bank of Cape Fear opened in the town in 1807; the State Bank of North Carolina opened there in 1810; an office of the Bank of the United States did likewise in 1817; and the Bank of Fayetteville joined the others in 1835. The Bank of Clarendon later supplanted the branch facility of the Bank of the United States. The county's prominent families supplied officers and employees for these institutions.

Taverns and Hotels

Cumberland's colonial distinction as a center of hospitality—
a place of taverns, inns, and "ordinaries"—continued in the
antebellum period. Thirteen such places were licensed between
1788 and 1790. Among them were the well-known Colonel James
Moore's on Rowan Street in Fayetteville; the older McIver's in the
Sandhills near Long Street Presbyterian Church; and Gilmore's,
four miles north of Fayetteville. In 1852 there were seventeen
"retailers" of liquor in the county.

Road and river travelers in 1825 had their choice of four
hotels in Fayetteville—the brand-new Lafayette, the older Planters
and Mansion hotels on Hay Street, and the Eagle on Gillespie
Street. In 1834 four places of public accommodation existed in the
town: the Jackson Hotel at Liberty Point, the Planters Hotel, a
new Lafayette Hotel, and the boardinghouse and stable of Hiram
Brockett. Four hotels were listed in the census of 1860, with an
average of twenty guests counted at each one.

JACKSON HOTEL,
LIBERTY POINT,
FAYETTEVILLE, N. C.
::::::::::::::::
The subscriber having leased the
above establishment in the Town of Fayetteville
gives notice to the public in general that it is now
open for the accommodation of Boarders and
travellers. His table will be supported with the
best fare which our market affords—His Bar
room with the choicest Liquors, in short every
exertion will be made to render his patrons com-
fortable. Particular attention will be paid to the
Horses of those who may favor him with a call.
From his determination to please all if he can, he
hopes to gain as well as merit a share of public
patronage.
THOS. H. MASSEY.
Fayettevile, Sept. 1st, 1834.—27tf.

This advertisement for Fayetteville's Jackson Hotel appeared in a
Fayetteville newspaper in September,
1834. Copy of advertisement supplied
by the author.

Labor

The small coterie of antebellum artisans in the county
periodically banded together in attempts to improve their bargain-
ing power. A "Mechanical Society" was chartered in the 1790s

under "an act for the relief of decayed mechanics." In 1834 the "master tailors" of Fayetteville announced an agreement to charge fixed rates for their work. In that same year, the Fayetteville Mechanics and Benevolent Society was chartered. Within five years its membership included 5 tailors, 3 carriage and wagon-makers, 3 carpenters, 2 coopers, 2 wheelwrights, 2 shoemakers, a saddler, a printer, a confectioner, a hatter, a plasterer, a blacksmith, a cabinetmaker, and a tinner.

Forest Products

Forest products—lumber, tar, turpentine—continued as a bedrock of the Cumberland economy. Firm information on production and sales is scarce, however. In 1824, 100,000 barrels of tar were shipped from Fayetteville to Wilmington. In 1840 Cumberland was said to have produced $78,540 worth of forest products, "the largest in the state." The popularity of turpentine (crude turpentine was quoted at $2.25 a barrel in 1849) helped improve local economic conditions before the Civil War. By 1860 scores of small turpentine distilleries and several larger units were in operation, although the industry was said to have "peaked in 1856."

These early engravings show workers engaged in the manufacture of turpentine, an important early industry in Cumberland County. Engraving at left courtesy North Carolina Collection; at right from the files of the Division of Archives and History.

Textiles

Cumberland County's little-known role as a pioneer antebellum textile-manufacturing district is a richly documented chapter of North Carolina industrial history. As early as 1803 William McClure signed up eighteen investors in a scheme to establish a "manufactory for carding, spinning, and weaving of cotton in the town of Fayetteville." The venture evidently was not successful.

In 1826, however, the textile industry was under way with construction in Fayetteville of the fourth cotton factory in North Carolina. By the 1840s the story included one of the state's first factory villages, a tiny settlement surrounding the Rockfish Manufacturing Company and the Beaver Creek Manufacturing Company—the present town of Hope Mills. The Rockfish factory, with 120 workers, was described as "the largest such establishment south of Petersburg." By 1860 it and a half-dozen other factories in Cumberland employed more than 550 workers and consumed 6,000 bales of cotton a year to make yarn and sheeting. It transformed the county into "the primary cotton processing and manufacturing place in the state before the Civil War," in the estimation of a modern-day historian of the industry.

The work force in these small factories consisted largely of girls, boys, and young women, whose size and agility were useful on the spinning line, where it was necessary to scramble under low-lying machinery to repair broken threads or untangle snarls. A few older men were needed to manhandle the bulky looms, known as "mules." Others operated and repaired the complicated leather-belt machinery powered by the waterwheel.

At first, textile manufacturing was seen primarily as a means of providing work for the most destitute segment of white society. Such workers were scorned by members of agricultural or artisan classes as "factory slaves." There is some evidence that the county's first factory operator utilized slave labor for a brief time. As the Civil War approached, however, the small industry began to exhibit the values of paternalism and civic virtue that came to characterize the postwar textile boom in the South. All but one of the little factories were destroyed during the war. But they left a tradition—social and economic—that became the foundation of the postwar industry in the county.

A firsthand description of Cumberland County's first factory, a rare document of industrial history, was provided in the summer of 1826 by the editor of the *Fayetteville Journal*, who visited the site of the facility, then under construction. Under the headline "Cross Creek Cotton Factory," he wrote that the building, "80 feet in length by 40 breadth" and three stories high, was located "just below [the confluence of] Cross Creek and Blount Creek." The mill was to be equipped with 1,000 to 1,200 spindles. The editor continued:

Mr. [Henry] Donaldson [the builder-operator] expects to put 400 spindles to work in a week. The spindles put in immediately will probably spin 150 pounds [of cotton] a day. The building is finished throughout in a plain and simple way. It will spin cotton of various sizes. It will employ 30 white boys and girls, of 12 upward. Pay $40 a year. And, in addition to the workers, there will be artificers [workers with special skills]. This to the poorer classes of people in this community will be of essential service, and we really rejoice in these times of scarcity and economic distress, that a way is opened in which the industrious poor can find profitable employment. This is now the 4th cotton-factory in the state and Donaldson started three! Every success!

Henry Donaldson (d. 1856), the state's pioneering textile factory builder, had joined with the Battle family in the early 1820s to erect two factories on the Tar River near Rocky Mount. In Fayetteville he joined two local investors—merchant George McNeill (d. 1865) and lawyer-politician Robert Strange, who had acquired the former gristmill site with an eye to cotton manufacturing.

Almost before it commenced operations, the factory was battered by a summer "freshet" that washed out milldams on every creek. Although the factory (with its machinery) was valued at more than $12,000 in 1829, financial difficulties forced it to close the following year—at which time Donaldson moved to Raleigh. It later reopened and operated until 1865, when it was destroyed by Union troops under General W. T. Sherman.

The longer-lived Rockfish Manufacturing Company was launched in 1837 by investors allied with the Mallett family, led by Charles Peter Mallett, who later sent his son, Charles Beatty Mallett, to New England to work and study in factories and with machinery firms. An 1840 eyewitness account by a local editor described Rockfish as a wooden building 175 by 55 feet containing 1,500 spindles and 100 looms, with the latest waterpowered machinery made by "the Matteawon establishment of New York." The mill utilized "1,500 bales of cotton per annum" to turn out "domestic" sheeting that sold for 8 to 10 cents a yard. Another 1840 report enumerated 14,234 spindles in Fayetteville, 20,110 in Richmond, Virginia, and 190,000 in Lowell, Massachusetts.

In 1843 *Niles Weekly Register* enumerated twenty-five cotton factories in North Carolina and six in Cumberland County. These six were: the Rockfish and the nearby Beaver Creek mills in present-day Hope Mills; a "Phoenix Factory" on Cross Creek at Ann Street, located within 300 yards of the

Market House in Fayetteville; the rechartered Cross Creek Factory in the town; a Mallett Mill on Blount's Creek; and, at a former gristmill site on Lower Little River near present-day Spring Lake, the "Manchester Factory" of the Murchison family. Total capitalization of these six facilities was $375,000. These same factories were operating just before the Civil War—Rockfish with 112 employees, Beaver Creek with 112, the others with fewer than 100 each.

The demographic characteristics of the people who toiled in these small factories can be inferred from data included in the 1860 census. More than 200 people gave their occupation as "factory hand," "yarn packer," "spinner," or simply "cotton mill." The work force was 90 percent female or teen-aged male, although some entire families—such as that of Felix Runnel, his wife, and two young daughters—labored in the cotton mills. Arthur Guin listed eleven members of his family as mill hands—including one male child age five. Susan Hilliard listed seven daughters as factory employees. The names of the sixteen-year-old Butler twins—Sally and Betsy—described as "factory hands," were listed next to that of Duncan Murchison, patriarch of the factory-owning family, who styled himself a "merchant-manu-facturer."

Frederick Law Olmsted, who visited the factories in 1854, wrote that most of the workers employed there were young girls from Scottish families. Although they evidently were quite poor, Olmstead reported that "in modesty, cleanliness, and neatness of apparell," these girls compared favorably with others he had observed in Glasgow, Scotland. Ten years earlier, there apparently were enough male workers employed at the Mallett mill to influence an election. Charles Mallett was accused by local Democrats of forcing his "factory slaves" to vote for Whig party candidates for public office.

Other Manufacturing

Hats, carriages, saddles and other leather products, turpentine stills, pottery, furniture, guns, watches, and paper were among other products manufactured in Cumberland County. The colonial hat factory of James Gee was continued by his family into the 1850s. A short-lived stoneware pottery factory on the brow of Haymount operated by merchant Gurdon Robins employed ten workers in 1820. The carriage factory of A. A. McKethan (1809-1890), often described as the largest in the South, was located in two brick buildings at the corner of Dick and Person streets in Fayetteville. In 1856 it employed seventy workers and "shipped 20 [custom-made] buggies to southern states in the last 12 months." Just across Person Street was the harness and saddle shop of free black Matthew Leary. The paper mill of David Murphy on Rockfish Creek near the Wilmington road made newsprint for Fayetteville newspapers. It was burned by invading Union troops in 1865.

A local historian, Quincy Scarborough, has published a roster of antebellum "artists and artisans" in Cumberland that includes 8 artists; 5 gunsmiths; 4 potters; 27 cabinetmakers, joiners, and chairmakers; 4 house and ornamental painters; 7 metalworkers; 3 tinsmiths; 25 silversmiths and watchmakers; 3 upholsterers; 2 stonecutters; and "numerous apprentices and negroes." The colonial tradition of manufacturing beer and hard spirits continued. In 1799 "the Brewery, at the foot of Hay Mount on Cross Creek," offered the "best beer in bottles," in barrels, or in gallons. An 1859 advertisement for a town whiskey dealer enumerated the brands he had for sale: "Dew-Drop, Magnolia, Family, Excelsior, and Reserve." The advertisement concluded: "We have other common brands of whiskey, but none are the 'long range,' such as Coffin, Rifle, Monumental, Blue Ruin."

Newspapers

Cumberland County was well served by antebellum journalism. One, and often two, newspapers were published in Fayetteville each year from 1789 to 1860. At least ten papers were published during the period, beginning in 1789 with the *North Carolina Chronicle & Fayetteville Gazette*; six years later this journal was being printed "under Franklin's Head [a sign in the shape of a silhouette of Benjamin Franklin] on Green Street." John Sibley, a politically active physician, was its founder.

In 1796 William Boylan founded the *North Carolina Minerva and Fayetteville Advertiser* but moved it to Raleigh three years later. During the next fifteen years at least six other short-lived weeklies were started. In 1816 Francis W. Waldo launched the *Carolina* (later *Fayetteville*) *Observer*. This journal was taken over in 1825 by young Edward J. Hale, a Chatham County native who was a printer and writer for newspapers in Raleigh and Washington. It became a leading political journal, with Hale as a major spokesman for the Whig party. The Democratic party had its Fayetteville voice in the *North Carolina Journal*, launched in 1827, which became the *North Carolinian* in 1839 and was issued as a daily just prior to the Civil War. By then, both the *Observer* and the *North Carolinian* published news received by telegraph. Telegraph lines were first brought into Fayetteville in 1847.

The Civil War

When it happened in the first days of March, 1865, Sarah Louise Augustus was a slave child. Sixty years later she could recall the events clearly:

> The Yankees came through Fayetteville wearing large blue coats with capes on them. Lots of them were mounted, and there were thousands of foot soldiers. The southern soldiers retreated, and then in a few hours the Yankees covered the town. They busted into the smokehouse on Marster's, took the meat, meal, and other provisions. Grandmother pleaded with them, but it did no good. They took all they wanted. They told us we were all free. The Negroes began visiting each other in the cabins and became so excited they began to shout and pray.

Sarah Louise's memories illustrate why the Civil War in Cumberland is a chapter best told in reverse. For history, as for her, those were the unforgettable hours during which the four-year conflict became a hearthside reality.

In one week, March 9-16, 1865, General William Tecumseh Sherman's army of 60,000 ragged Union veterans (Sarah Louise's memories of neat coats and capes may have been influenced by later lithographs) tramped through the rain-soaked cotton fields and pinewoods of the county, paused for a weekend of careful destruction in war-weary Fayetteville, and then marched out. On March 16, a day's march from the town, retreating southern troops dug in at the rural crossroads of Averasboro on the Harnett County line and fought a noisy delaying action. Nearly 200 men on both sides were killed in this next-to-last clash at arms in North Carolina. Then the war moved on from Cumberland. Its end was only hours away.

As General Sherman and his men entered the county at the end of a five-week march from Savannah, Georgia, he wrote his commander, General Ulysses S. Grant: "We have swept the country well. The men and animals are in fine condition." Sherman's troops, preceded by swarms of undisciplined "bummers" and supplied by hard-bitten foraging parties, were already legendary for their grim success in making real a remark uttered by Sherman during a dinner party a few months earlier: "War is cruelty. There is no use trying to reform it. The crueler it is, the sooner it will be over."

Setting out on February 1, Sherman aimed for Fayetteville, expecting to link up with other Union troops moving inland from Kinston and recently captured Wilmington. He also intended to destroy the arsenal, one of the last remaining sources of arms for the dying Confederacy. As the bluecoats streamed north, small units of Confederate cavalry and artillerymen routed from the Charleston garrison fell back to join a tiny army assembling under General Joseph E. Johnston.

By the second week in March, the Confederates were in Fayetteville, where they dug trenches along the Raleigh road. Soldiers and slaves also enlarged a formidable earthen redoubt that had been erected in August, 1863, at the southeastern foot of the Clarendon Bridge over the Cape Fear River. On March 9 the arsenal's machinery was dismantled, hauled away on the railroad, and hidden within the shafts of the Egypt Coal Mine in Chatham County. In the early hours of March 10 at Buie's Farm, or Monroe Crossroads, on what is now the Hoke County line, Confederate cavalry of Lieutenant General Wade Hampton's command overran the sleeping headquarters camp of Union Brigadier General Judson Kilpatrick's cavalry. The twenty-nine-year-old Union commander escaped in his nightclothes, then rallied his troopers to retake the camp. The action soon earned an enduring nickname: "Kilpatrick's shirttail skedaddle."

On the morning of Saturday, March 11, there was more shooting within sight of the Market House as a small party of Confederates, among whom was General Hampton himself, surprised a patrol of Union cavalry. Eleven Union soldiers were killed, a dozen captured. In a few hours, however, Hampton was gone, having burned the Clarendon Bridge behind him. The main

In March, 1865, Union troops under the command of General William T. Sherman entered Fayetteville (*top*), where they captured the Cumberland County Courthouse (*center*) and an area near the Market House (*bottom*). Engraving and line drawings from *Battles and Leaders of the Civil War*, Volume IV: *The Way to Appomattox* (New York and London: Thomas Yoseloff, 1956), 691, 679, 690.

body of Sherman's army then trooped in. By nightfall Archibald McNeill, mayor of Fayetteville, had formally surrendered the town, and Sherman's forces were camped on the grounds of the arsenal, in fields, yards, streets, and even in gardens and orchards. Then the town, so accustomed to fire, saw it again.

On Sunday morning, March 12, in a letter probably written from the arsenal grounds, General Sherman informed General Grant of his intentions for the facility: "Since I cannot leave a guard to hold it, I therefore shall burn it, blow it up with gunpowder, and then with rams knock down its walls." The razing was done by Michigan engineers under the direction of Brigadier General Orlando M. Poe, before the war a designer of fortifications, now adept at destroying them. And so, wrote eyewitness Alice Campbell years later: "The nights were made hideous with smoke. The crowning point to this nightmare of destruction was the burning and battering down of our beautiful and grandly magnificent Arsenal, which was our pride, and the showplace of our town."

There was additional destruction. Union Brigadier General Absalom Baird, who was named military governor of the town for the army's stay, reported: "Before leaving the town, I destroyed 2 foundries of some importance, 4 cotton factories, and the printing establishments of 3 rebel newspapers." By the following Tuesday the Union columns were on the move, crossing the Cape Fear on a temporary pontoon bridge. By Wednesday evening they were gone. A day more, and the sharp engagement in the farm fields and pinewoods at Averasboro left scores of southern wounded to be cared for at plantation houses.

The Beginning

The story had opened four years earlier. As in North Carolina generally, Cumberland people in early 1861 were reluctant to leave the Union. A call for a convention to consider secession failed in a statewide referendum on February 23. Cumberland voters divided almost evenly.

President Abraham Lincoln's call for 75,000 troops on April 15, 1861, changed all that. Seven days later a scratch force of volunteers from militia companies commanded by Colonel John H. Cook, following instructions from North Carolina governor John W. Ellis, marched up to the arsenal and called upon its commander, Captain James Bradford, to surrender the facility to the state. Bradford did so, hauling down the Stars and Stripes and raising a North Carolina flag. Bradford soon joined the southern army as an artilleryman, died of illness in 1863, and was buried on the arsenal grounds.

Within a few weeks several hundred young men left farms or factories or stores to join companies of volunteers forming in the county. The new Cape Fear River steamer *A. P. Hurt* was kept busy ferrying these raw recruits to Wilmington, where they took railroad cars to regimental gathering places near Raleigh or Weldon. By autumn the county had heard of the first actual fighting by its soldiers—and of its first deaths, mostly from illness. Several more companies of volunteers were being formed. On Haymount, the arsenal was being busily prepared for its wartime role.

Soon the weeks of preparation would turn to months, then seasons, then years of casualty reports, of increasing cost in blood and treasure, of dwindling hopes. The most vivid eyewitness account of these years is the diary of a teen-ager, Melinda Ray of Fayetteville, a journal filled with sad details of funerals and reports of battle casualties. A typical entry: "James Huske was killed near Petersburg Oct. 27th. He has been in the war since the commencement of it. His mother, a widow, is left desolate. She had two sons three years ago, and now they are both gone."

In the spring and summer of 1864, following the bloody battles of the Wilderness, Spotsylvania, and Cold Harbor, the *Fayetteville Observer* printed column after column listing casualties in every state unit and special notices of the scores of Cumberland County men killed, wounded, or captured. That autumn the home front also became increasingly dark, despite editor Edward J. Hale's unflagging editorial zeal for the southern cause. Confederate army deserters were reported to be stealing horses in the county. Two others were remanded to neighboring Harnett County to be tried for murder. Graham D. Baker, Esq., was convicted of "distilling whiskey from grain," a wartime offense inasmuch as flour had become scarce. He was fined $5,000 and given a sixty-day jail sentence. A Cumberland County colonel stationed in Virginia published a "Notice to Absentees," urging men on furlough from the regiment to report back to ranks "depleted in many battles." Mourning the dead, a "Monument Association" convened in September, 1864, to raise money for a suitable memorial in Fayetteville.

The hardships caused by shortages and dwindling markets were exacerbated by the continued decline in the purchasing power of Confederate money. In 1865 bacon that had sold for 10 cents a pound before the war was priced at $6.00 a pound. Fayetteville's important prewar banks closed one by one. Relief efforts by state and local governments attempted to ease the suffering. According to one calculation, fully 40 percent of the women in Cumberland received such help in 1864. In early 1865, as Wilmington fell to Federal forces and Sherman's army approached Fayetteville, the town's two-story Ladies Seminary, converted to a hospital a year earlier, became busier than ever. There, the town's few remaining physicians, aided by women volunteers, cared for convalescent wounded and sick soldiers right up until the day the bluecoats marched in.

The closing scenes of the war provoked vivid recollections. J. M. Rose, a farmer who resided near Fayetteville, wrote:

The Federal soldiers searched my house from garret to cellar, and plundered it of everything potable; took all my provisions, emptied the pantries of all stores, and did not leave me a mouthful of any kind of supplies for one meal's victuals. They took all my clothing, even the hat off my head, and the shoes and pants from my person. They destroyed my furniture and robbed all my negroes.

A Federal officer and commander of General O. O. Howard's artillery provided the Yankee perspective on Cumberland's condition. While in Fayetteville with Sherman, Major Thomas Osborn wrote his brother: "The town contains perhaps three thousand people, is old and timeworn. It has probably been a fashionable town, but now looks old and rusty. The country surrounding the town is as poor as the Lord could well make it."

Men at Arms

The county provided eight initial companies of Confederate troops. Scores of other volunteers and conscripts were added as the war went on. It is calculated that from one fourth to one third of the white males of the county served in southern ranks. Two militia units—the Fayetteville Independent Light Infantry and the Lafayette Light Infantry—went into service with the First North Carolina Regiment, the "Bethel Regiment," which fought the first skirmish and suffered the first casualty of the war near Big Bethel Church, Virginia, on June 10, 1861. The Lafayette later became an artillery unit: Company B of the Thirteenth North Carolina Battalion, known as "Starr's Battery" for Captain Joseph B. Starr, its commander and later a lieutenant colonel. It served in eastern North Carolina throughout the war.

The "Cumberland Plowboys," an infantry company under the command of Captain Jonathan Evans, became Company F of the Twenty-fourth North Carolina Regiment. Company E of the Eighth North Carolina Regiment was raised as the "Manchester Guardians" in the northwestern part of Cumberland County by Captain James M. Williams. The "Carolina Boys" were Company K of the Thirty-eighth North Carolina Regiment, headed by Captain (later Major) Murdock McLaughlin McRae, age twenty-eight, a schoolteacher. It had the largest percentage of men with Highland Scots names of any unit in the southern army, and it fought with the Army of Northern Virginia in nearly every battle of the war. Seven of its men surrendered with Robert E. Lee at Appomattox. Captains Peter Mallet, O. H. Blocker, Francis N. Roberts, and Peter J. Sinclair also raised or commanded infantry troops from Cumberland.

Among cavalry units, Captain James W. Strange commanded Company D of the Second Regiment of North Carolina Cavalry, organized in 1861. Captain James H. McNeill, age thirty-eight, a Presbyterian minister, organized "McNeill's Company of Partisan Rangers" in 1862 and trained it at Blockersville (present-day Stedman). It became Company A, Fifth North Carolina Cavalry. Both companies were components of the Army of Northern Virginia. Late in the war McNeill became colonel of his battered regiment and was killed in action near Petersburg nine days before Lee's surrender.

Several Cumberland County men became combat colonels. The Murchison brothers—John R. and Kenneth R.—commanded the Eighth and Fifty-fourth North Carolina regiments respectively. John was mortally wounded at Cold Harbor, Virginia, in June, 1864; Kenneth was captured in late 1863 and spent the rest of the war as a prisoner. H. A. McKethan commanded the Fifty-first North Carolina Regiment in the same brigade (Clingman's) with the Eighth.

While hundreds of men lived to return to peacetime lives, several score died in battle or of wounds, and scores more succumbed to disease. Not all the casualties were Confederate, however. Fayetteville postmaster John MacRae had four sons in the southern forces. A fifth, Alexander MacRae, was among a handful of professional soldiers from the South who stayed in the United States Army and died wearing its uniform. MacRae, an

1851 graduate of the United States Military Academy at West Point, New York, died in hand-to-hand combat on February 21, 1862, while defending his artillery battery at the battle of Valverde in the New Mexico Territory. "The most heroic death in the national army was his," according to one tribute. MacRae's body was reinterred in the United States Military Academy Cemetery at West Point.

The Home Front

Home-front war activities consisted of recruiting, supporting the arsenal and local troops, and periodic collections of clothing and comforts by Sheriff Hector McNeill, who forwarded the collected items to North Carolina soldiers. Confederate victories were celebrated with bell ringings and church services. Somber newspaper notices and funeral services lamented defeats and deaths. The columns of the *Fayetteville Observer* reported a wide range of war-related activity. The Cumberland Hospital Association regularly raised funds to be sent to military hospitals in Richmond and elsewhere. The Young Ladies Knitting Society advertised for wool "to knit gloves for the soldiers." Farmers were told where to bring produce to be surrendered as "tax in kind" in lieu of the rapidly depreciating Confederate currency. Conscript officers listed places at which men could register for Confederate service.

The Arsenal

Beginning the day Captain Bradford hauled down the United States flag, the Fayetteville arsenal became significant to the Confederate war effort. At the time, thousands of old muskets were stored there. Eighty or ninety workmen under the direction of architect-superintendent William Bell, who like Bradford had cast his lot with his adopted town and the Confederacy, immediately began repairing the weapons and making ammunition.

In October, 1861, machinery salvaged from the United States armory at Harpers Ferry, Virginia, arrived, and manufacture of weapons began. From then until William T. Sherman's army approached Fayetteville in February, 1865, the Fayetteville Arsenal and Armory, as it was officially designated, sent a steady supply of rifles, pistol carbines, ammunition, knapsacks, and artillery carriages to the battlefronts. More than 200 workmen labored in the arsenal's sheds, shops, enginehouses, and forges. Women—both volunteers and a few who were paid wages—kept records, sewed accouterments, and cooked for the garrison and work force.

The work force included former white employees of the Harpers Ferry armory, slaves, and free black artisans. There was a small garrison, as well as a volunteer company that manned a defensive earthwork at the mouth of Rockfish Creek; the earthwork was named "Fort Booth" for Major John C. Booth, "Commandant of the Arsenal" until his death in September, 1862. The garrison later consisted of a small battalion known as the "Arsenal Guard" under Lieutenant Colonel Frank Childs, a prewar acquaintance of General Sherman. The arsenal advertised for large supplies of "blackjack wood" and sought "fishermen, good at taking sturgeon" to augment rations. The garrison voted 82 to 5 for Zebulon B. Vance over W. W. Holden in the gubernatorial election of 1864.

In 1865, when General Orlando M. Poe's bluecoat engineers smashed and torched the more than twenty structures comprising the Fayetteville Arsenal and Armory, William Bell, then age seventy-two, watched as "the most important work of his life" disappeared in fire and smoke. "The shock was extreme," wrote his biographer, "and he never recovered from it." Bell died six months later. For another fifty years, shattered stones from the ruins of the armory were used as building material in walls and houses erected in Fayetteville after the war. Some foundations of arsenal structures were still in place 125 years later.

CHAPTER SEVEN

Between the Wars: 1865-1918

Cumberland County in the fifty-three years between the Civil War and World War I was a typical southern rural place. It changed slowly with the times as the nation went through transformations wrought by emancipation, invention, and the end of the frontier. Most people lived on farms. Life centered on work, family, church, and visits to a nearby small town. By 1900 the coming of railroads cracked open the door of isolation.

Fayetteville remained a small courthouse village with life revolving around commerce, family, the minimal county government, and church. Many townspeople worked in small textile plants and resided next to their workplaces in look-alike cottages of a factory village. The town's gentry—a small circle of landowners, professionals, and merchants—lived in large Victorian houses on tree-shaded streets off the Market Square or on the heights of Haymount. Their children attended privately financed schools or, beginning in the 1880s, small graded schools financed by public appropriations. A few young men went off to the university at Chapel Hill or to Wake Forest College.

Black citizens, who comprised half the population of the town, increasingly included families reaching for new middle-class status. From the moment the Civil War ended, schools for black children sprang up. The leaven of education slowly created new opportunities, despite the racial cleavage and white domination that marked the period. By 1900 these black citizens were among the first generations of former slaves and children of former slaves who moved into such professions as teacher, preacher, lawyer, or physician. Like many offspring of white families, many of them left their birthplace to make a life elsewhere. The large majority of black people, however, were farmers, sharecroppers, laborers, loggers, domestic workers, turpentine distillery workers, or lumber mill employees. A rare glimpse of one of these unsung people is provided in an obituary notice inserted in the *Fayetteville Observer* in 1916 by a white man. The notice read:

> Died at his home in Cedar Creek at 11 a.m. today. Andrew Melvin, aged about 88 years. He was a turpentine distiller by trade for the last 45 years. . . . Andrew was faithful, upright, and true, a good neighbor. He wielded a noble influence for good among his race and others in his community. We will miss him, but believe his soul is at rest.

Racial segregation became more and more entrenched during the period, although the influence of such local black leaders as educator E. E. Smith (d. 1933) and James Walker Hood (1831-1918), senior bishop of the African Methodist Episcopal Zion Church, ameliorated some of the harsher expressions. Blacks and whites joined in celebrating when Vice-President Levi P. Morton and John Philip Sousa's famous Marine Band came from Washington to Fayetteville for the 1889 centennial of the ratification of the United States Constitution.

In this period, social life changed from the rural and village mode to a more complex, modern one—from the days when the newspaper announced "picnics for the small fry at Eccles Pond" (1867) to train excursions, an annual agricultural fair, traveling circuses, the opening of the era of jazz, the Victrola, and the moving picture.

Organized sports grew in popularity. The first baseball team in Cumberland, probably one of the first in the state, took the field in the spring of 1867, with the editor of the *Fayetteville Eagle* commenting: "As it [the game] will not be allowed to interfere with what little business anybody may happen to have, its results will be beneficial." The following year the "Lafayette team" was playing host to a club from Wilmington. In 1909 the Fayetteville Baseball Company fielded a professional team known as the Highlanders. In 1914, during an exhibition at the county fairgrounds, a skinny new player with the Baltimore Orioles blasted a home run—his first in professional baseball—350 feet in the air "over a fence and landed in a corn field." The career of George Herman (Babe) Ruth had begun.

The isolation of rural life was ameliorated by railroads as crossroads communities sprang up along the lines. In their heyday

Fayetteville's citizens commemorated Confederate Memorial Day in 1909 in typical fashion with a parade. Photograph from picture postcard in the possession of Stephen E. Massengill, Raleigh.

at the turn of the century there were thirty-nine rural locations with postal service in the county, as compared to nine in the mid-1870s. Many of the names have disappeared from the land, but in 1897 they were Alderman, Antonia, Argyle, Beard, Brunt, Buckhorn, Carlos, Carmichael, Cedar Creek, Clay Fork, Cornelia, Cumberland, Dial, Edonia, Falcon, Fayetteville, Floyd, Gillisville, Godwin, Grays Creek, Hope Mills, Idaho, Inverness, Kyles Landing, Leavitt, Little River Academy, Manchester, Montrose, Pike, Raeford, Rhodes, Robin Hill, Roslin, Sherwood, Starsburg, Stedman, Vander, Wade, and Wicker.

The 1890s brought political turmoil as fusionists seized control of local government from long-dominant Democrats. There was also momentous social change: the end of the saloon in 1897, followed in 1901 by total prohibition. Legal liquor would be gone for thirty-six years. The change prompted a new industry. Manufacture of bootleg whiskey became a major occupation in swamps and forests along the Cape Fear River and Rockfish Creek.

For many years, certain holidays in Fayetteville were marked by what could charitably be called high spirits. It was a custom as old as colonial muster days. In 1868 a local newspaper declared: "Christmas was a time of riot!" On Christmas Day,

1900, however, "public order was almost perfect," the *Fayetteville Observer* reported. The new year 1901 was ushered in with "Remsburg's Fine Orchestra in uncommon good form [playing] in the elegant rooms of the Pythian Lodge on Market Square." The three-story lodge, erected by the Knights of Pythias in 1893, was one of the town's finest buildings, reflecting the growing popularity of civic clubs and organizations. Dancing was a custom as old as the county. In 1867 it was reported that during "the hop at Fayetteville Hall . . . there was good order, sweet music, pretty feet, and graceful movement."

In this period, Cumberland had a noteworthy literary chronicler in Charles Waddell Chesnutt (1858-1932), a pioneer black novelist and short-story writer who grew to young manhood in Fayetteville. He utilized scenes of his youth in his writing, describing "Patesville," a fictional village that was his hometown in all but name. The following passage from Chesnutt's short story "The Goophered Grapevine" is true to the facts and the mood of the place:

> A quaint old town. There was a red brick market-house in the public square, which held a four-faced clock that struck the hours. There were two or three hotels, a court-house, a jail, stores, offices. While Patesville numbered only four or five thousand inhabitants, of all shades of complexion, it had a considerable trade in cotton and naval stores. This business activity was not immediately apparent to unaccustomed eyes. Indeed, when I first saw the town, there brooded over it a calm that seemed almost sabbatic in its restfulness, though I learned later on that underneath its somnolent exterior the deeper currents of life—love and hatred, joy and despair, ambition and avarice, faith and friendship—flowed no less steadily than in livelier latitudes.

All was not placid, however. In the 1890s there were frequent threats of violence in political campaigns. Lynching parties were not uncommon. There were brief strikes at textile plants in 1909 and 1915, outbursts from the tensions always lurking just below the surface in the small factory villages. By then, too, racial animosity was at a peak. Novelist Chesnutt commented from his Cleveland, Ohio, home that "race prejudice was more intense and uncompromising than at any time since emancipation."

Sensational incidents of crime, often with harsh racial overtones, caused periodic alarms. Most notorious was the 1900 trial and hanging of Louis Council, a young black man convicted of raping a young white woman in his rural neighborhood. Despite widespread doubts concerning Council's guilt and even an

Charles Waddell Chesnutt (1858-1932), who spent his formative years in Fayetteville, later became a nationally recognized author of novels and short stories, many of which dealt with the problems encountered by persons of mixed race. He is recognized as the first African-American writer to receive serious attention for his literary attainments. Photograph reproduced courtesy Western Reserve Historical Society, Cleveland, Ohio.

appeal from the sheriff of Cumberland County, Governor Charles B. Aycock refused to spare him. Clutching a crucifix and protesting his innocence, Council was hanged in the small Victorian jail in Fayetteville. The fact that the sheriff, the judge, and several others connected with the case died violently within a few years of the hanging created legends that lingered for generations.

Within a one-year period in 1907-1908 two police chiefs of Fayetteville were gunned down, one at his Sunday dinner table. The killers, both black men, were hastily tried and hanged in the jailhouse. One defendant was brought into court lying prone on a stretcher, in a coma from allegedly battering his head against the jailhouse bars. Nevertheless, the trial proceeded.

Population Perspective

From 1870 to 1910 Cumberland's population doubled, approximating the pace of population growth in the state at large. The 1870 census enumerated 17,035 people in the county, a few hundred more than in 1860. More than 44 percent were black, and for the first time the county's black residents were listed by family name. In 1880 black citizens comprised 47 percent of the county population of 23,836, a historically high percentage. By 1910 the total population of Cumberland had reached 35,284, of which 43 percent were black.

Fayetteville had a different experience. Between 1860 and 1900 the town's population remained static, hovering just below that indicated in the 1860 census and never reaching 5,000. Fayetteville's population, 4,790 in 1860, surpassed that figure again only in 1910, at 7,040. The black population generally comprised just less than half the total, peaking at 49.7 percent in 1870.

Reconstruction

Within a few weeks after Union troops marched away in March, 1865, the Civil War was over. Scores of former Confederate soldiers drifted back to farms and villages, straggling home from battlefronts and northern prisons. They found weed-grown cotton, soggy bottomlands (a flood, dubbed "Sherman's Freshet," sent the Cape Fear out of its banks even as the bluecoats marched through). Fayetteville was scarred by fire and destruction. There was no money and little trade. There was also a momentous social change: legal slavery was no more. Black and white were testing new ways of dealing with each other and attempting to discern what the future would hold.

Several Fayetteville black men emerged as leaders of the freed community. After attending a convention of freedmen at Raleigh in the summer of 1865, they urged cooperation between the races in Cumberland County. But returning Confederates were pressing for a virtual return to the antebellum status quo. Isham Sweat, a free black barber who attended the freedmen's convention and later played an important role in the county's politics, described the situation in an October, 1865, conversation with a traveling reporter:

When Sherman's troops were first taken away from Fayetteville, and the town was put in the hands of its citizens, they showed a disposition to revive the slave code, and to enforce certain city ordinances that were full of the old spirit; Negroes were not to be allowed to meet together for worship, unless a white man was present in the assembly; no Negro was to carry a walking cane, etc.; one man, after being convicted of some offense, was publicly whipped.

Blacks decided against asking for a garrison of federal troops and instead sought help from the Freedmen's Bureau. Sweat and others went to Wilmington, secured some satisfaction concerning enforcement of the offending ordinances, and brought back promises of emergency food supplies for blacks and whites.

Nonetheless, tensions grew in 1866. Confederates observed the May anniversary of General "Stonewall" Jackson's death as a town holiday. They complained of "restless negroes." Blacks sought permission to parade on July 4, but town officers refused. The Freedmen's Bureau intervened again and won approval for a small observance of Independence Day.

The following year brought radical change. In 1867 the mild Reconstruction program of President Andrew Johnson was replaced by congressional Reconstruction, more vigorous in its determination to enfranchise black people and more determined to enforce new federal laws promoting political and economic opportunity. The United States army took control of state politics until elections could be held under a new constitution. Many former Confederates were disenfranchised, even as former slaves were encouraged to become voters. This turn of events ushered in a brief period during which black citizens played leading roles in public affairs.

The Republican party held a county organizational meeting on April 9, 1867, in Fayetteville's "Farmers Hall." The son of black patriarch and harness maker Matthew Leary was elected chairman. The Reverend James W. Hood of Evans Chapel Methodist Church, the Connecticut native who was later assistant state superintendent of schools, presided. Soon a military garrison arrived to police the town during the upcoming elections. Company K of the 8th Regiment of U.S. Regulars was comprised of black soldiers and white officers. It used the Dobbin Hotel on Hay Street as a barracks. On July 4, 1867, a crowd of 2,000, mostly black but with a few whites, observed Independence Day by parading on the main streets of Fayetteville. Some marchers, black and white, wore their blue uniforms as veterans of the Union army.

That same summer 1,505 whites and 1,439 blacks in the county, including 483 whites and 707 blacks in Fayetteville, registered as new voters. Under the newly promulgated congressional Reconstruction plan, Provisional Governor W. W. Holden named to the Fayetteville town board a number of interim local officials, including three black men: Matthew Leary, Jr.; Lewis Lomax, a minister; and Andrew Jackson Chesnutt (1833-1920), a Fayetteville native who had emigrated to Ohio, served as a teamster in the Union army, and returned to his hometown.

In 1868 Holden was elected governor, and the Republican party gained control of the North Carolina General Assembly. Two black men from Cumberland served 'as members of this body: John Sinclair Leary (d. 1908), youngest son of Matthew Leary and later head of the law school at Shaw University in Raleigh, and Isham Sweat, previously identified. Matthew Leary was elected to the county board of commissioners, the new body constituted to assume the powers of the now-defunct court of pleas and quarter sessions. White "carpetbaggers," former Union soldiers who had settled in the county, were named to courthouse jobs—sheriff, clerk of court, register of deeds. Governor Holden visited Fayetteville in September to meet with the new office-holders and voters. The gathering was noteworthy in that it included "106 colored men and 14 colored women," a rare instance of female involvement in nineteenth-century politics.

This high tide of Reconstruction quickly receded, however. By 1870, in an election decided by fewer than 200 votes, former Confederates reclaimed the state legislature and numerous court-house offices under the banner of the so-called "Conservative" party. The former Confederates were triumphant again in 1872, this time under the banner of the renascent Democratic party. In 1873-1874 the Republicans made a last stand in county elections. By this time, some native white leaders—including Captain Ben Robinson (b. 1843), a popular Confederate veteran and scion of a prominent Fayetteville family—had become Republicans, having been won over by the party's advocacy of grass-roots democracy and public education. The *Statesman*, a weekly newspaper launched by Robinson in April, 1873, was an unusually evenhanded and factual party journal. It was notable for its articles pointing out accomplishments by black citizens.

A noteworthy interlude occurred on April 11, 1874, when black and white citizens assembled to mourn the death of Nelson Henderson, an eighty-three-year-old barber and longtime bands-man for antebellum militia units. Henderson was buried with full military honors. It is likely that some of the black mourners wore their Union blue uniforms and that some of the whites wore their Confederate gray to his funeral.

The acrimonious political atmosphere of Fayetteville per-sisted. Ben Robinson ran for mayor of the town and lost by a single vote, although Republicans won four of seven ward seats on the town board. That autumn, however, Democrats swept to victory in all contests. They went on to win every successive election for the next twenty years. The *Statesman* soon published its last issue. Reconstruction had come and gone.

The Howard School

Although the political ascendancy of freed slaves and other black citizens was brief, a more lasting fruit of Reconstruction was the beginning of organized public education for black children. The first schools for the children of freed slaves in Cumberland County opened in the autumn of 1865 under the auspices of the Freedmen's Bureau and the American Missionary Association (AMA), a northern philanthropic organization. In October of that year the Freedmen's Bureau reported the existence in Fayetteville of three schools with eight black teachers and 198 students. In February, 1866, there were three schools with two white teachers and 263 pupils.

By the summer of 1867 a visiting AMA official looked in on two Fayetteville schools and reported that one, operated by two black men from Ohio (the Harris brothers, Robert and Cicero, natives of Fayetteville), assisted by a black woman from the town, was "an excellent school, one of the best in the state." The official concluded: "The attendance is large and regular and the teaching thorough and complete." Another such facility, operated by the Episcopal church, had "a positively discouraging" record. "There is no discipline, little study, less teaching and pretty nearly no progress," the AMA official wrote.

At the time, the Harris school was located in the old Evans Chapel church building on Cross Creek. That summer, the school operated by the Harris brothers was officially renamed the "Howard School" for General O. O. Howard, head of the Freedmen's Bureau. Five black men paid $150 for a tract of land on Gillespie Street, and construction began on a building to house the school. The deed was signed by A. J. Chesnutt, then proprietor of a grocery store; David Bryant, a farmer; and three ministers—Robert Simmons, Thomas Lomax (later a Methodist bishop), and George Granger. In June, 1868, the white editor of the *Index* visited the school, still in Evans Chapel, and wrote that he was "much pleased" at the "220 scholars" and "the brothers Harris." He reported: "A large building is under construction on the southern outskirts" of Fayetteville to house the facility.

Robert Harris, one of North Carolina's most admired black teachers of the Reconstruction era, died in 1880. By then the school had been given a $2,500 state appropriation (1877) and designated as the "State Colored Normal School," in which teachers were to be trained. Harris was succeeded by his most notable student, Charles W. Chesnutt, who left after three years for New York and Cleveland, where he later became the nation's first important black novelist and short-story writer. Chesnutt was succeeded by young E. E. (Ezekial Ezra) Smith of Goldsboro, a minister-teacher who headed the school for fifty years until his death in 1933 (with time off as United States minister to Liberia in 1888 and for military service in the Spanish-American War).

Until the twentieth century, the Gillespie Street building housed both the teacher-training school (in three rooms on the top floor) and Fayetteville's school for black children (on the first floor). For a few years after 1900 the school was located on "Ashley Heights," off Robeson Street, near a silk-making factory that employed only black workers. A rented building on Worth Street also housed the school for a brief period. In 1905 Smith prevailed on the legislature to appropriate funds for a building.

These eleven students comprised the class of 1904 at the so-called "State Colored Normal School," successor institution to the "Howard School" of the immediate post-Civil War period and forerunner of present-day Fayetteville State University. Photograph courtesy Fayetteville Publishing Company; supplied by the author.

Meanwhile, he purchased a 42-acre tract of land on Murchison Road. In 1908 Aycock Hall, named for former governor Charles Brantley Aycock, was in use.

Politics

After the unique but brief period of Reconstruction, county politics mirrored that of the state. Democrats won every election from 1870 until the 1890s, but Republicans—including many black voters—were always a significant minority. In 1884, 1,219 blacks and 1,794 whites paid poll taxes.

A succession of lawyers and businessmen represented the county in the legislature (two seats in the state House of Representatives and one in the state Senate). Only seven of these legislators served more than a single term. George M. Rose, a railroad lawyer and Confederate veteran from Fayetteville, was Speaker of the House in 1883 during his third term. Thomas Sutton, a lawyer and president of a cotton factory, was in the House for four terms. W. C. Troy, a merchant, served in the Senate, 1870-1872, 1876, and 1885. In 1913 the county's representation shrank to one seat in the lower house and a Senate seat shared with other counties.

The Democratic grip was broken briefly in the 1890s when Populists—discontented farmers who had joined the Farmers' Alliance—formed coalitions with Republicans and won state and local elections on a "fusion" ticket. In 1892 Republican and Populist candidates for governor together outpolled Democrat Elias Carr in Cumberland. In 1894 Cyrus Murphy, a farmer-teacher from the Flea Hill community (Eastover) and a respected Confederate veteran, was chairman of the county Populist convention, which met to choose its candidates and plan for fusion with Republicans. In county and legislative elections of 1894, the fusion ticket, including Murphy as candidate for clerk of court, swept every office. The vote was extremely close, however. Murphy won, 2,227 to 2,180, over his Democratic opponent. Warren Carver, a longtime Republican elected to the state Senate, vowed to sponsor a constitutional amendment for a ten-hour workday.

In the 1896 election fusionists again won all county offices. But in 1898 the Democrats concentrated on race as a campaign issue ("Have We Negro Rule?" asked a campaign advertisement) and narrowly wrested control of local offices from Murphy and the other winners of 1894 and 1896. The first rally of the "Red Shirts," white men extolling white supremacy and warning blacks against participation in politics, was held at Fayetteville on October 21, 1898. In the 1900 election for governor, following another full-blown white supremacy campaign, Democratic winner Charles B. Aycock received 2,719 votes in Cumberland to 1,629 for Republican Spencer B. Adams.

After a disfranchisement amendment to the state constitution was ratified in 1900, political activity by blacks was curtailed, and many older Republican and fusion activists died or eschewed politics. Campaigning was confined to intraparty battles among Democrats, particularly after party primaries were implemented in 1912. By 1916 only 631 whites and 205 blacks paid poll taxes.

Cumberland's most important state political figure of the period was Ralph Potts Buxton (1826-1900), son of a longtime Episcopal rector. Buxton was a superior-court judge (1865-1874), mayor of Fayetteville (1857), member of an anti-secession convention, and Republican candidate for governor of North Carolina in 1880. As a student at the University of North Carolina in the 1840s, he expressed the sentiment that blacks should be free, and throughout his life he held views that upheld education, the rights of blacks, and economic development. Buxton, a mentor to generations of lawyers and politicians, had "a clever but delicate sense of humor."

During a distinguished career, Ralph Potts Buxton (1826-1900) served as an attorney, mayor of Fayetteville, a state solicitor, a delegate to the state constitutional conventions of 1865-1866 and 1875, and judge of the North Carolina Superior Court. He was the unsuccessful Republican candidate for governor of North Carolina in 1880. Engraving from *Historical and Descriptive Review of the State of North Carolina . . .* (Charleston, S.C.: Empire Publishing Company, 1885), 189.

Government

In these years, government scarcely touched the lives of the great majority of people. Until 1900 the small government revenues, derived principally from poll taxes and levies on property, went for modest courthouse expenses, to maintain a few indigents, and—in small amounts, voted and levied by separate districts—for schools. The valuation of assessed property remained at approximately $3 million from 1864 until about 1889. Even in 1899 it was only twice what it had been during the Civil War.

By 1916 county government had a more modern character. Property was valued at $6.9 million—$4.7 million in land and $2.2 million in personalty. Property owned by whites was valued at $6.4 million; that owned by blacks, at only $659,000. Fayetteville, which had accounted for one third of the total property valuation of the county in the nineteenth century, accounted for $4 million of the $7 million total county valuation in 1916.

In 1894 the crowded 100-year-old courthouse was replaced by a small but elegantly designed new structure in the popular Gothic Revival style, complete with corner tower, at the intersection of Russell and Gillespie streets in Fayetteville. A tiny jail was located

FAYETTEVILLE, N. C.   Court House

This attractive Gothic Revival-style structure, erected at the corner of Russell and Gillespie streets in downtown Fayetteville in 1894, served as Cumberland County's fifth courthouse until 1925, when it was replaced by a newer facility. The 1894 edifice was razed in the 1950s. Photograph from picture postcard held by Duke University Manuscript Department, Durham.

behind the courthouse. Inside the open well of the jail, the county's last public executions by hanging were carried out, with the condemned falling from scaffolding attached to a second-story railing.

The public buildings were surrounded by the noisome pens and barns of mule dealer Charles Bevill ("the mule king of the South"), who advertised that he regularly purchased Missouri animals in lots of 500. Fayetteville was an important livery market at a time when every few acres of cotton required a plow mule, when the mule and cart was a main mode of transport, and when the log woods rang with the crack of the teamster's whip.

Mules and courthouses could not coexist, however, especially during summer. The already cramped courthouse was replaced thirty-one years later by a handsome marble-encased structure girdled by a frieze of chiseled moral slogans. Immediately criticized as an extravagance, the new courthouse would remain in use for a half-century. It did solve the mule problem, however, being located on the former site of Bevill's main barn.

To serve the legal and administrative needs of a courthouse town, Fayetteville always had a well-stocked stable of lawyers. Sixteen attorneys resided in the town in 1867 and in 1896, and thirty-four lived there in 1916. After 1900 the county constructed an up-to-date "county home" for the indigent. A new county health officer created a furor by temporarily banning produce sales at the Market House. Farm extension work commenced in 1914, and public welfare services began to be offered in 1917.

Fayetteville municipal government had more extensive responsibilities: maintaining streets, bridges, and ditches; building water and sewerage lines (1889); paying part-time policemen; and maintaining the old "Town House" as a market (downstairs) and municipal office (upstairs). The town surrendered its municipal charter in 1881 under a legislative act to "compromise the indebtedness" (escape paying for a series of bonds issued in the 1870s). A full charter was not reenacted until 1893. During the interim, however, other legislative acts provided for election or appointment of town officials, divided the town into four wards (in lieu of the seven of antebellum years), and authorized taxing powers. At least part of the reason for the surrender of the charter was political and racial, rather than economic. By reducing the number of wards and allowing the General Assembly to name some town officials, the surrender enabled whites to control

This engraving, based on a pen-and-ink sketch, shows Fayetteville's Green Street, looking north, about 1889. From *Fayetteville Observer*, Illustrated Trade Issue, June 27, 1889.

municipal affairs at a time when black voters were almost as numerous as whites. Even after Reconstruction, blacks occasionally had been able to elect town officers under the original ward system. Former black legislator John Sinclair Leary was a town commissioner in 1877.

Following restoration of the town charter, annual elections again took place. William S. Cook served as mayor of Fayetteville, 1893-1902, and James D. McNeill (1850-1927) held the office for six years between 1910 and 1919. McNeill was a leader in the statewide movement for professionally trained fire fighters and was for many years fire chief in Fayetteville. With his walrus moustache and booming voice, McNeill, owner of the last waterwheel mill on the Newberry mill site beside Cross Creek, was the town's most notable character in the early twentieth century. Another was Captain A. B. Williams (1843-1904), whose Confederate artillery battery was said to have "fired the last shot at Appomattox." Williams served as mayor, chairman of the county commissioners, and chairman of a committee to make arrangements to celebrate the 1889 centennial of North Carolina's ratification of the United States Constitution.

In 1905 a "Public Works Commission" was created. It took charge of water and sewer systems and the retailing of electric power. In 1908 town officers, firemen, and police moved from the Town Hall to a two-story building on Gillespie Street. Policemen got uniforms, and the fire department abandoned horse-drawn equipment for gasoline-powered vehicles. Street paving (described proudly as the "bithulithic process"), a new "abattoir," and electric lights were added.

Other Towns

In spite of the proliferation of rural crossroads communities in the 1890s and the early twentieth century, Fayetteville remained the only place in Cumberland County with an appreciable municipal government. Incorporation laws were passed for several communities in the county: Wade in 1889; Hope Mills in 1891; Manchester in 1895; Godwin in 1905; and Stedman (known earlier as Blockersville), Falcon, and Linden in 1913. Only Manchester had as many as 1,000 citizens in 1900, and these communities' minimal municipal governments were defunct by the 1920s, except in Hope Mills.

This photograph of the railroad depot in the southwestern Cumberland County town of Hope Mills was made in 1914. Photograph supplied by the author.

Hoke County Created

Burgeoning population encouraged landowners and merchants in western Cumberland—principally Quewhiffle Township—to seek a new county centered on the town of Raeford, which had been incorporated in 1901. The new county, named Hoke, was created in 1911. More than 8,000 citizens, including many Scots Highlander families, resided in the new county.

Education

For thirty years after the Civil War, schooling resembled that of the antebellum years, except that now black children were involved. Rude one-room buildings, often made of logs, provided the setting in which a young teacher, sometimes only a year or two older than the oldest pupils, taught reading, writing, and ciphering during a school season that lasted a few months in fall and winter. Better-off families sent children to private academies, which often employed but a single teacher. Fayetteville also had a military academy during several decades of the period. Preachers, both black and white, frequently doubled as teachers.

After 1900 Cumberland entered the new era of larger "graded" schools and of more generous public support for education. School terms were lengthened, teachers better trained. Nevertheless, the marks of the old order lingered in rural areas of the county until World War II, especially for black children.

The Freedmen's Bureau schools had an impact on education for whites, as described by Alexander Graham (1844-1934), a Fayetteville native known as "the father of the graded school in North Carolina." Graham wrote:

In 1878, in lower Fayetteville, there was a difficulty between two white men one Sunday afternoon, and they were tried in the Market House on Monday. Six white boys and six colored boys were witnesses. At the end of the trial, the six colored boys signed their names, and the six white boys could not write. All Fayetteville was looking on when this happened. The people were greatly disturbed. They did not blame the Negroes but they blamed themselves. They did not wait for the Legislature to meet. Everybody subscribed from five cents up to $250. They made up a fund of thirty-five hundred dollars and elected teachers.

Graham, a teacher and Confederate veteran, was chosen head of the new school financed by the subscriptions. By the late 1880s the new facility had more than 500 students and was supported by taxes. Graham became superintendent of Charlotte's public schools in 1888 and subsequently gained a statewide reputation. His son, Frank Porter Graham (1886-1972), a native of Fayetteville, became president of the University of North Carolina, 1931-1950; United States senator, 1949-1951; and an official of the United Nations.

In the 1880s the one-room schoolhouse proliferated. An 1884 report listed "35 white and 25 colored" schools in the county, as well as the "free graded schools" in Fayetteville. County school revenues that year totaled $7,497. In 1900 these were the official statistics: 5,305 white children taught by 77 teachers and 4,741 black children taught by 57 teachers. There were 10 "log" schools for white children and 3 for black children, 40 frame buildings for white children and 38 for black children. The high school movement, in which Alexander Graham was a leader, came to Cumberland shortly after 1900. High schools for white children were established in Hope Mills, Stedman, Godwin, and Eastover in 1909.

Following passage of a $50,000 bond issue in 1910, three new brick schools—Central, Person Street, and Haymount—were built for the white schoolchildren of Fayetteville. In 1911 Fayetteville became a separate school unit known as "The Fayetteville Graded Schools." Black children in the town got their first modern school in 1915 when the "handsome new building" of the Orange Street School was completed. The two-story brick structure remained in use for thirty-eight years. In 1916 town schools reported a total enrollment of 1,067 children. Orange Street School was already filled to capacity, with 853 children enrolled and more than 500 in attendance daily. The total school budget for the town was $16,000. In that year, the county board of education named committees for no fewer than 103 individual schools. The county school appropriation for the year was $13,600.

A leading educational figure in the early twentieth century was John A. Oates (1870-1958), a lawyer, newspaper publisher, state senator, and county judge. Oates was chairman of both the Fayetteville and the Cumberland County school board; in these capacities he backed bond issues and boosted educational improvements. As a state senator in 1917 he introduced a pioneering anti-illiteracy bill and later served as a member of the state board of education.

Women and Civic Action

Women were not permitted to vote until 1920, but they played important roles in a series of civic events during the early twentieth century. The newly organized United Daughters of the Confederacy flowered. An early project was successful in 1902 when a statue honoring heroes of the Lost Cause was erected at the north end of Green Street. Even earlier, in the 1890s, Fayetteville women organized the "Monday Afternoon Club," later known as the Haymount Book Club, which has been described as "the first literary organization in North Carolina." Over coffee and cake they discussed local needs and issues, as well as such topics as "The Danube River and Its Relation to Present-Day Affairs." In 1889 women wrote and edited a special "Woman's Edition" of the *Fayetteville Observer*, emphasizing the issues of civic reform and betterment.

When in 1907 it was proposed that the seventy-five-year-old Market House be razed so its site could be used by Fayetteville's first United States post office, the town's leading women flew to arms at a mass meeting. After they had successfully defeated the proposal, they formed a permanent "Women's Civic Association," which subsequently evolved into the Fayetteville Women's Club and remained active in the realms of library service, beautification, and historic preservation. Many of the same women joined Mrs. Josie Hunter Smith in convincing the North Carolina General Assembly to finance a home for widows of Confederate veterans. The home was erected in 1915 beside the route of the old plank road west of Fayetteville, along which William T. Sherman's bluecoats had tramped into town fifty years earlier.

In this period a few women engaged in commerce. Mrs. M. E. Dye was a milliner in 1867; Lizzie Mallett dealt in "millinery and fancy goods" in 1877; Mrs. L. R. Dye did likewise in 1897. Women were the proprietors of half of the county's hotels and inns.

Churches

After the Civil War, churches proliferated in countryside and town and for both the black and white citizens of the county. Black people—both former slaves who had attended white services and antebellum free blacks—organized Methodist (1865), Baptist (1872), Episcopal (1873), and Presbyterian (1874) congregations in

Fayetteville. Falling Run Missionary Baptist Church, a congregation of freed slaves, was organized in 1872 in Cedar Creek Township under William DeVane and Ransome Royal. Savannah Baptist Church was established by former slaves in 1873 just across a cotton field from Cumberland Union Baptist Church, a white congregation. Beauty Spot Missionary Baptist Church was organized in 1875 in the Flea Hill community.

Bishop James Walker Hood, the Connecticut-born black preacher who settled in Fayetteville, organized several dozen congregations of the African Methodist Episcopal Zion church in the region. In 1893 the Evans Chapel congregation in Fayetteville erected a handsome brick building at the site on which cobbler-preacher Henry Evans had raised his slab-board chapel ninety years earlier. In 1896 black Episcopalians in Fayetteville moved into an elegant shingle-style church structure notable for its Tiffany glass windows; the building was financed by the philanthropy of Mrs. Eva Smith Cochran (d. 1909), a carpet-industry heiress from Yonkers, New York, who wintered in Cumberland County at the turn of the century.

The congregation of St. Patrick's Catholic Church erected a house of worship on Bow Street in Fayetteville in 1829. This structure is a remodeled version of the 1829 church building as it appeared at about the turn of the century. Photograph courtesy Duke University Manuscript Department; supplied by the author.

By 1885 there were 51 churches in the county, among which were 20 Presbyterian (1 black), 15 Methodist (3 black), and 10 Baptist (1 black) congregations. In 1900 there were more than 70, including 30 black congregations. In prosperous times after 1900, white Fayetteville congregations replaced their plain antebellum frame churches with Victorian-style structures; examples include the First Baptist Church in 1906 and Hay Street Methodist Church in 1908.

The religious ferment of post-Civil War days saw the birth of new denominations. The Pentecostal Holiness church had its national roots in rural Cumberland. The Campbellton (Person Street) Pentecostal Church dates from 1898. In an oddly shaped wooden "octagon tabernacle" in the crossroads of Falcon, the Reverend A. H. Butler (1875-1963) of that church presided in 1911 "where Fire Baptised and Holiness churches consolidated to form the Pentecostal Holiness Church."

Health Care

The tradition of noteworthy medical practitioners carried over into the years between the wars as medicine progressed toward modern ways. Eight physicians practiced their profession in the county in 1867, and sixteen did so in 1916. In Fayetteville one of North Carolina's earliest modern hospitals was built in 1896 on the corner of Hay and Green streets by Drs. Frank Highsmith and J. H. Marsh; the facility was enlarged in 1906 to fill the block. In 1904 Marsh built St. Luke's Hospital, one of the last of the old-style medical facilities, on Haymount. The angular, rambling wooden structure lasted only a few years. A pioneering black physician, Dr. C. A. Eaton, converted a black-owned Hillsborough Street hotel into a "sanatorium" in 1914.

The tradition of public health care had its first twentieth-century expression as the county appointed a part-time health officer. When a smallpox scare swept Fayetteville in 1901, the board of aldermen ordered compulsory vaccination and established a "pest house," where suspected victims were examined and inoculated. Despite these advances, the great majority of people lived and died with little attention from medical practitioners. The Highsmith hospital did not even admit black patients until Mrs. Cochran, the New York heiress, bought a residence next door to the facility, had it refurbished as the "Cochran wing," and designated it for use by black and indigent sufferers.

Several notable druggists carried on another tradition by marketing, and in some cases manufacturing, popular patent-medicine nostrums. W. C. McDuffie, Jr., S. J. Hinsdale, H. R. Horne, T. W. Broadfoot, and B. E. Sedberry were active in their state professional organization. Sedberry's fashionably styled three-story "mansard roof" store and manufactory was built in 1883 on Person Street near the Market House, where it stands at the present time. The town had two pioneering black druggists— Frank Williston and Robert Holiday.

Agriculture

In the years between the wars, cotton continued its reign as king of agriculture and was more central to the economy than ever. An average of 12,000 acres—20 percent of the county's cleared land—was planted in cotton. Yields, which fluctuated with the vagaries of weather and market conditions, averaged 5,000 to 6,000 bales annually. The price of cotton trended downward in

Fayetteville's importance as a commercial center for the marketing of agricultural products can be inferred from this early twentieth-century view of numerous mule-drawn wagons loaded with bales of cotton near the town's Market House. Photograph from picture postcard postmarked 1908; supplied by the author.

relation to the cost of living: 26 cents a pound just after the Civil War, 10 cents in 1880, 6 cents in 1890, and 17 cents in 1916.

The cotton crop required many hands. Freed slaves often became tenants on the plantations on which they had dwelt before the war. The tenancy rate hovered at 50 percent. A majority of farmers tended small acreages, and few had more than one or two tenants. In the 1920s a third of the county's black farmers owned their land. The Eastover (Flea Hill) section east of the Cape Fear was a center of black farm ownership. Cotton provided livelihood for others besides farmers. In the early twentieth century a dozen cotton gins—half of which were in Fayetteville—processed the crop. Fertilizer, implements, and seed sales were important, and it was the heyday of the mule dealer.

Corn, raised mainly for fodder, was the major user of land, requiring about half of the county's 60,000 to 80,000 open acres of land available from 1880 to 1915. It was milled at a dozen gristmills in the county. Hogs were of major importance. Approximately 20,000 head were reported in farm censuses. Pork was the staple of country diets. Hog killing was a typical farm chore. There was also a brisk butchering business in Fayetteville. The number of cattle, largely grown for local consumption, averaged more than 7,000 head. Until 1900, sheep were also important, with more than 5,000 counted each year.

Fish from the Cape Fear River, principally shad, were caught in nets and weirs, "cured" with salt, and consumed in large quantities. Regular sale days for pork, fish, and beef were mandated at the Market House in Fayetteville, creating problems in the days before refrigeration. A turn-of-the-century county health officer issued stern rules against the sale of "stinking fish" and other products left too long in stalls.

Transportation

Cumberland's long-frustrated dream of joining the railroad age—fifty years old by 1880—was finally realized in the 1890s when the Cape Fear & Yadkin Valley Railway was extended beyond its pre-Civil War terminus at the Egypt coal mine into piedmont North Carolina. The CF&YVRR erected a handsome depot in Fayetteville in 1883, with the yards and a roundhouse located beside the main tracks east of Hillsborough Street. By the 1890s, major routes of the Atlantic Coast Line system ran through Fayetteville. Near the turn of the century, three depots stood

In this ca. 1910 view from a picture postcard, travelers await the arrival of a train at Fayetteville's Atlantic Coast Line depot. Photograph courtesy Fayetteville Publishing Company; supplied by the author.

nearly side by side in the town. The ACL depot at the corner of Hillsborough and Hay streets (erected in 1893) was replaced in 1911 by a larger structure that remains in use at the present time.

On the River. As the railroad became transportation king, the riverboat entered its final era of importance on the Cape Fear. In 1867 at least five paddle-wheel steamers operated on the Fayetteville-Wilmington run—the *Gov. Worth* and the *A. P. Hurt* of the Cape Fear Steamboat Line; the *North Carolina*, owned by merchant J. Lutterloh; and the *R. M. Orrell* and the *Halcyon*, owned by merchant A. M. Orrell. In the 1890s, with railroads taking over much of the freight business, the Cape Fear and People's Steamboat Line was still operating the *A. P. Hurt*, which departed Fayetteville every Monday and Thursday at 7:00 A.M. and returned from Wilmington on Tuesdays and Fridays. Other vessels operated on the Cape Fear in that period included the *D. Murchison*, the *North State*, the *Wave*, the *Marion*, the *Cape Fear*, and the *R. E. Lee*.

The design of these small vessels was basic: flat bottom, shallow draft, a superstructure topped by a deckhouse and a tall stack, a large name board hung proudly alongside the wheelhouse. Most of the cargo placed aboard these ships included cotton, turpentine, lumber, wheat, and tobacco. Passengers lounged in rooms on the superstructure or strolled the narrow decks. The

The *Cape Fear* was one of several steam vessels that plied the Cape Fear River in the late nineteenth century, conveying freight and passengers between Fayetteville and Wilmington. In this view the paddle-wheel steamer is berthed near Fayetteville. Photograph from Robert Preston Harriss Papers, Duke University Manuscript Department; supplied by the author.

steamers came upriver loaded with merchandise to be sold by Fayetteville merchants. Few seasons passed without a scheme to combine railroads and river trade to transform Fayetteville into a commercial metropolis. But neither were there many years during which the fickle Cape Fear did not fall too low or rise too high for vessels to complete their voyages on schedule.

In 1903 *The City of Fayetteville* (the second vessel of that name), regarded as the finest steamer ever to ply the Cape Fear, went into service. This boat, built in Jacksonville, Florida, specifically as a passenger carrier, boasted fourteen first-class staterooms, a six-foot-wide promenade deck, and "electric push-buttons, lights and water throughout." A total of 137,000 tons of commercial cargo—largely wood products and fertilizer—was shipped via the Cape Fear above Wilmington in 1908. During that year a flood sent the river swirling almost to the Market House, and the United States Army Corps of Engineers constructed two locks on the lower river designed to control the flow.

Nevertheless, by the early years of the twentieth century the days of the riverboats were numbered. When *The City of Fayetteville* commenced its overnight runs between Fayetteville and Wilmington in 1903, railroad bridges were already spanning

In this 1909 photograph a coal-fired steam locomotive of the Cape Fear & Yadkin Valley Railway chugs across the Cape Fear River railroad bridge south of Person Street on its way into Fayetteville. By this time the railroad had supplanted the riverboat as the chief means of transportation in Cumberland County. Photograph supplied by the author.

the river, and steel-and-concrete highway bridges would soon follow. The elegant vessel sank at Wilmington in 1913 when its steel hull broke in two under the weight of a load of cotton bales. When the old *A. P. Hurt* burned and sank near the same spot in 1923, two centuries of riverboat history came to an end.

Automobiles. After 1900 a few vehicles powered by the internal combustion engine were braving the dirt-track roads of the county. An early photograph of an automobile, made in 1902, depicts Wade T. Saunders, Sr., of Fayetteville and his family posed in his Philadelphia-made car. Another photograph, made ten years later, shows the Market House square; nearby appears a pioneer motorcycle tended by its unidentified rider. In 1913 the county's first "graded" road was completed, linking Fayetteville with Hope Mills. By 1915 nearly all the "hacks," one- or two-horse canopy-covered buggies that had carried passengers around Fayetteville, had been supplanted by automobiles. During the decade of the 1920s the automobile became king of the jazz-age road. In 1920 traffic cops were already a major item in Fayetteville's budget. By 1923, of 179 warrants issued by the Fayetteville police department in one month, 126 were for motor vehicle violations.

Communications

When William T. Sherman's army marched out of Fayetteville in 1865, the town's lively publishing industry was a wreck. Union troops had smashed the presses of the *Fayetteville Observer*, the three-month-old *Daily Telegraph*, and the *North Carolina Presbyterian*. Edward Jones Hale, the fiery editor of the *Observer*, left for New York, where he and his sons established a book-publishing firm that was soon noted for its titles of wartime autobiography by prominent former Confederates. For the ensuing fifteen years, Cumberland readers got their news and political views from a succession of short-lived weeklies, as well as from the *Presbyterian*, which resumed publication for several years after the war.

In 1883 Edward Joseph Hale (1839-1922), son of Edward Jones Hale and formerly a Confederate officer, returned to

Edward Jones Hale (*left*) and his son Edward Joseph Hale (*right*) were Cumberland County's two principal contributions to the field of journalism and publishing. The elder Hale edited and published the *Fayetteville Observer* the town's leading antebellum newspaper, from 1825 until the journal's offices were burned by Union troops in 1865. The younger Hale was affiliated with his father and brother in a New York City publishing firm in the period following the Civil War. In 1883 he returned to Fayetteville and successfully resumed publication of the *Observer*. Photographs from the Albert Barden Photograph Collection.

Fayetteville and resumed publication of the *Observer*, after having acquired new type and presses. J. H. (Harry) Myrover (1843-1908), another young Confederate veteran who had worked for the *Observer* before the war, edited several of the weeklies in the 1865-1883 period and subsequently rejoined the staff of the *Observer*. The Myrover family continued to produce journalists whose bylines graced the *Observer* until 1965.

One unique journalistic production was the *Fayetteville Educator*, published weekly for fifty-two editions in 1873-1874 by William Caswell Smith (1856-1937). It was North Carolina's first black-owned newspaper. Smith, born to slave parents in Cumberland, was a teacher before learning the printer's trade. He later moved to Charlotte and edited the *Charlotte Messenger*, another pioneering black journal.

During the Civil War the *Fayetteville Observer* had received "war news" by telegraph on a daily basis. The first telephone was installed in Fayetteville in 1894, with Miss Sallie Atkinson as the first operator hired. Initially there were but six customers of telephone service.

The Textile Industry

The array of small, water-powered factories—at Rockfish (later Hope Mills), Manchester, and Fayetteville—that had made the county significant in antebellum textile manufacturing was a victim of Sherman's army. Only the Beaver Creek mill in Rockfish was spared the torch, because, according to legend, its superintendent was native to the Massachusetts town of the Union troops detailed to set it afire.

The industry soon bounced back, however. Cumberland never again ranked with such burgeoning textile-producing areas as Alamance or Guilford counties; but textile manufacturing continued to be important to the economy, and the factory village was a significant social setting. While the earlier factories were launched and financed largely by local enterprise, the postwar additions often resulted from joint enterprise of noted state textile barons, particularly the Holt family of Alamance County, in alliance with professional textile operatives and local investors. Near the end of the nineteenth century, the older factory village at Rockfish, renamed Hope Mills, was joined by a new district just outside Fayetteville that took the name "Massey Hill" for the family that had owned a crossroads country store nearby. Massey

Hill's district sprang up in 1898 around the new, 10,000-spindle Holt-Morgan plant (which was sold in 1917 to Puritan Mills). In that year, a company financed by the Holt family also built on Russell Street in Fayetteville a 5,000-spindle plant known as Holt-Williamson, which was still in operation in the 1980s.

Steam was replacing waterpower in these up-to-date plants, and it was soon followed by electricity. Villages of typical workers' cottages were built around the factories. By then, the factories in the Hope Mills area included Hope Mills Manufacturing (14,600 spindles), Beaver Creek and Bluff (a total of 3,800), and Cumberland Mills (3,000). The Hope Mills firm's "Cotton" plant (named for the owner, S. H. Cotton) had replaced waterwheels with water-turned turbines. The small 2,800-spindle factory at Manchester on Lower Little River, twelve miles north of Fayetteville, was by then known as "Murchison Mill," having been named for the family that had launched it sixty years earlier.

In 1900 there were two notable additions to the local textile culture. First was "The Happy Village of Tolar-Hart," built on 190 acres of the former McIntyre Brick Yard just up the ridge from the Holt-Morgan plant in Massey Hill. The two-story

The Lake View Cotton Mill was located in the Massey Hill industrial district, which came into being in 1898 on the outskirts of Fayetteville. Photograph from picture postcard held by Duke University Manuscript Department.

factory and its surrounding cluster of cottages became something of a model for paternal industrial operations and remained a family-owned enterprise until the 1940s. The owner, John Tolar, hired two full-time community workers—Ollie Vick Livingstone and Lucy Currie. Livingstone left a journal of her work as a teacher of night school and kindergarten, home economics adviser, librarian, club organizer, and builder of communal spirit. The "happy village" (a name used in advertising and even in song) had its own small library, community hall, Episcopal chapel, playground, baseball field, and tennis court. When several members of the "Happy Family" went off to World War I, the company honored them by having their names cut on a small stone monument set on the grounds of the factory office.

Despite the paternal atmosphere, Tolar-Hart employees worked long hours for the low wages of the time. "Families had from five to seven children," wrote one observer, "and most of them worked in the mill, until the child labor law was enforced." One mill worker reported in 1896: "We have a public school here, but the factory people cannot spare their children from the mill to attend it. They are too poor. If they were to send them, it would be against the wishes of the managers to do so, as they need the children's labor in the mill." Pay rates were 58 to 83 cents a day for men and 40 to 75 cents a day for women.

This photograph of textile workers standing behind a loom was made inside the Bluff Mill near Hope Mills about 1908. Photograph supplied by the author.

Ollie Vick Livingstone's description of the workers' cottages is applicable to any of the cotton-factory villages: "Most of the houses had three large rooms. The long kitchen had a table and a stove at opposite ends of the room. The bedrooms were off the main room. At least once a week, the pine floors were scrubbed with corn shucks and lye soap. Each house had its own garden and most families had some pigs or chickens." Until after World War II the company owned the cottages. The Holt-Morgan plant rented its houses for 25 cents a room per month. A gala day for Tolar-Hart was March 20, 1920, when the village celebrated the installation of electric lights in workers' homes. The factory itself had been operating on electricity since 1901, paying $17.50 annually for its 300-horsepower load.

A final addition to the Massey Hill district was the Victory Cotton Company plant and village, completed in 1906. By then, the day of the waterwheel had passed. Steam, and then electricity, powered the machinery. The Victory plant was later known as Faytex; still later it was known as Lakedale.

The county's most noteworthy textile enterprise was the Ashley-Bailey Silk Company, whose silk-weaving factory was erected a mile from Tolar-Hart on Robeson Street in 1900. The company's two three-story brick structures were of the latest modern design. The silk mill was unique in that it employed only black workers, mostly women, at a time when the textile work force was virtually all white. The Philadelphia-based firm was convinced from its operations in Paterson, New Jersey, that black workers were better able to manipulate the slinky product of their looms. A superintendent who was himself black was sent from the company's New Jersey facility. The Ashley-Bailey silk factory was an early example of a pattern that soon became familiar—the flight of northern manufacturing to the low-wage South. By 1900 Fayetteville and Philadelphia were only hours apart via convenient passenger and freight railroad service.

In 1914 the factory reported 26,000 spindles and 472 looms, which processed 135 tons of raw silk a year and produced a finished product worth $375,000 annually. There were 310 female and 135 male workers. Wages ranged from 65 cents to $3.00 for a ten-hour day. An extensive factory village sprang up around the silk plants on "Ashley Heights," with street names such as "Italy," "Belgium," and "German" (all silk-making processes), as well as "Silk Lane." The company acquired hundreds of acres of pinewoods and ponds adjoining its factory sites. At the present time these rolling acres are Fayetteville's most exclusive country club and residential neighborhoods.

Trade

On June 29, 1865, Melinda Ray of Fayetteville wrote in her diary: "Two or three yankees have opened dry goods stores here. Benny Robinson has started a paper here the first number of which was issued yesterday." Commercial life was stirring in Fayetteville in the ashes of the Civil War. In 1867 the town's business directory listed approximately 70 merchants, 3 jewelers, 2 druggists, 3 hotels, and 2 boardinghouses. A. A. McKethan's carriage manufactory was still in business, and Mrs. M. Banks maintained her toy and confectionary shop. The 1877 business directory listed more than 120 merchants and tradesmen, 8 saloons, 3 hotels, a restaurant, 2 banks, a savings and loan company, and 2 hat shops operated by women.

Black tradesmen were also part of the antebellum commercial scene. All six of Fayetteville's bootmakers were black, and three of the town's four "eating houses" had black proprietors. Four of thirteen blacksmiths and wheelwrights were black, and three black men operated grocery stores. Barbering was still an all-black occupation; there were three in Fayetteville. Charles Bowen, a black man, was the town's only cabinetmaker in 1883.

By the 1890s the general stores that had dominated the mercantile scene since colonial days were being supplemented by a growing array of specialty businesses. The new-style department store arrived with the "Big Store" of Frank Thornton & Sons on Hay Street. Fayetteville's business directory for 1897 listed 150 businesses and tradesmen and 10 hotels and boardinghouses, including the Lafayette Hotel, erected in 1889.

By 1916 the town boasted its first mercantile "skyscraper," a five-story tile-roofed structure overlooking Market Square. The building was erected to house the Stein Brothers department store. Jacob and Kalman Stein, born in Lithuania, had operated commissaries in the South African outback before emigrating to America and going to Fayetteville in 1905. Their "Capitol" store eventually replaced Thornton's as the town's leading merchandising facility, and it remained under family control for the ensuing seventy years. The Steins were among a group of notable Jewish merchant families that joined Fayetteville's commercial life. Hyman Fleishman (1870-1934), an immigrant from Latvia,

In this "View of Hay Street, Looking West," ca. 1889 (*top*), some of Fayetteville's leading commercial establishments of that time are identified. The signs displayed over the entrances to the first two buildings at left bear the following names: "T. W. Broadfoot & Co.," "J. M. Beasley," and "Wm. Jackson." In the opposite view of Hay Street, looking east, about 1915 (*bottom*), the large structure at right is the Lafayette Hotel. Engraving from *Fayetteville Observer*, Illustrated Trade Issue, June 27, 1889; photograph from picture postcard held by Aubrey T. Haddock, New Bern.

arrived in 1908. His eight sons and a daughter remained active in the field of merchandising for another seventy-five years.

By 1916 Fayetteville's business directory listed more than 300 firms and individuals. There were such newcomers as bicycle shops (4), five-and-ten-cent stores (3), florists (2), and a Chinese laundry ("wah sing"). There were 3 banks and 2 savings and loans, a chamber of commerce, and 19 firms or individuals selling insurance. The traditional businesses persisted. There were 5 dealers in carriages, 8 mule and horse dealers. But automobiles were proliferating, and there were 3 "garages." Six hotels, as well as 9 inns or boardinghouses, served the traveling public.

Commerce in the surrounding countryside had been stimulated by the spread of railroad-stop villages in the 1890s. In 1897 more than forty businesses—mostly general stores—were scattered in such places. In 1916 the textile-factory town of Hope Mills boasted more than thirty businesses and tradesmen.

Turpentine and Forest Products

The distilled turpentine industry, which had begun in the 1840s, grew even larger after the Civil War. In 1867 there were twenty-one owners of small distilleries in the county. Among the

Turpentine and forest products, Cumberland's traditional commercial mainstays, remained important commodities well into the twentieth century. This tuprentine still stood alongside railroad tracks near Fayetteville. Photograph (ca. 1910) from picture postcard; from the files of the Division of Archives and History.

important distillers were Thomas C. Lutterloh, an antebellum founder of the industry, and A. H. Slocomb, a New Englander who arrived just after the war. As many as sixty-one small "stills" were in operation in the 1870s. By 1897 there were fifteen distilling operations, some of which, including Slocomb's, were of considerable size. Walter Watson's "edge-tool manufactory" in Fayetteville turned out distilling tools used by the industry throughout the South. In the 1880s Fayetteville reported receipts of 18,000 casks of distilled turpentine and 60,000 barrels of rosin. By 1916 turpentine operations were confined to three larger firms. Lumbering was then the major forest industry, with seventeen sawmills and fifteen lumber companies in operation in the county.

Other Manufacturing

At the conclusion of the Civil War, Cumberland County's manufacturing facilities were typical of the nineteenth century—harness, saddle, and carriage makers; crafters of farm implements and turpentine tools; a gunsmith; and barrel makers. By 1897 these craftsmen were joined by candy makers, beer distillers, brickmakers, bakers, machine tool makers, and the proprietor of a "cider works." There were also the Raiford brothers, makers of both sausage and candy, and the drugstore of Pemberton & Prior on Market Square, manufacturers and purveyors of "Prior's Rheumatic Remedy."

Vineyards and Wine Making

The sweet scuppernong grape grows well in the sandy soil of North Carolina's coastal plain, and wine making had been a plantation industry in that region since colonial days. In the 1880s and 1890s wine making flourished into a commercial enterprise. The "Tokay" vineyards and winery, located a few miles north of Fayetteville and owned by Colonel Wharton J. Green (1831-1910), Confederate veteran and congressman, were reputed to be the largest such enterprise "on this side of the Rockies." In 1896 a commercial directory indicated that 400 acres of land in Cumberland were devoted to the growing of grapes and that 100,000 gallons of wine were produced there annually. The advent of Prohibition halted the 35,000-gallon-per-year Tokay operation and also shut down the "Bordeaux" vineyards located west of Fayetteville.

Another important boon to Cumberland County's economy in the late nineteenth and early twentieth centuries was viticulture. These workers are harvesting grapes near Fayetteville. Photograph from picture postcard held by Duke University Manuscript Department.

Military Units

Soon after the Civil War the Fayetteville Independent Light Infantry and the Lafayette Infantry, the county's two principal antebellum volunteer militia units, were reorganized. In addition, an all-black unit, Company C, known as the "Howard Light Infantry" of volunteer militia, was formed. Many veterans of the Union army were members of this new unit.

Lieutenant Colonel Abraham Halliday (1835-1915) of Fayette-ville was commander of a three-company black battalion that included units in Raleigh and elsewhere. During the Spanish-American War in 1898 the Fayetteville Independent Light Infantry was called into national service as Company A, Second Regiment. It did not see action, however. Black leaders in North Carolina insisted that black citizens should also be allowed to serve in the Spanish-American War, and in response the Third North Carolina Regiment, the first all-black volunteer unit since the Civil War, was formed. E. E. Smith, principal of the Colored Normal School, was second-in-command of this unit. The

Fayetteville Independent Light Infantry was called up for a 1916 United States expedition to the Mexican border and spent several weeks in active service at El Paso, Texas.

Natural Events

Memorable weather-related events were also part of the era. In 1893 the Cape Fear River froze "from bank to bank." The river flooded in 1908, sending water swirling up to the central part of Fayetteville and threatening to wash away the 1865 wooden road bridge and the newer railroad bridge. In 1916 a "cyclone" demolished the grandstand at the fairgrounds and a wing of the new county home.

Fayetteville experienced one of its worst floods in 1908 when the Cape Fear River spilled over its banks and inundated portions of the town's business district. Photograph from picture postcard in the Ernest R. and Della G. Carroll Papers, State Archives.

World War I

When the United States entered the conflict against Germany on April 6, 1917, Cumberland County people became part of the First World War, "the war to end all wars." Several hundred went off to fight. Under the Selective Service Act, 3,379 county men were registered—2,180 white and 1,199 black. In April, 1917, the first draft quota called 222 men from the county. The Fayetteville Independent Light Infantry Company was called to federal service as Company F of the 119th Infantry Regiment, part of the Thirtieth Division. It fought in Flanders. Other young men were in the Eightieth Division, the Ninety-second, the Air Service, and various other units.

At home, civilians participated in Liberty Bond drives—the county's quota in the fourth drive was $780,000, an amount equal to twice the taxes paid to the county government in 1917. They joined the Red Cross to wrap bandages and prepare gift boxes for soldiers. They gathered at the railroad station to cheer as groups of draftees and National Guard units boarded for training camps. They worried about a wood shortage in the winter of 1917-1918 because so much of the lumber industry was devoted to the war effort. And they read about the war in the trenches, as the Doughboys of the Allied Expeditionary Forces joined the fight that ended with the Armistice on November 11, 1918.

For men from the county, the experiences in France were the most memorable of their lives. For some, they were their last. Private Cyrus Adcox, age twenty, from a family in the Holt-Morgan textile factory neighborhood of Massey Hill, was the first

Cumberland soldier "to die in the trenches" in France. The *Fayetteville Observer* reported that he was killed in action with the machine gun battalion of the Thirtieth Division on May 29, 1918, during some of the earliest fighting by an American unit. A memorial service in the factory village featured hymns by the church choir of the neighboring Tolar-Hart factory community.

On July 12, 1918, nineteen-year-old Robert Porcelli was killed in action with Company H of the 119th Infantry of the same division, the first soldier "from the municipal limits of Fayetteville" to die in battle. Porcelli, an Italian immigrant, had enlisted in the Fayetteville Independent Light Infantry in 1916 when only sixteen years of age and had gone with the unit to the Mexican border.

The first black man of Cumberland County to give his life had died earlier, on February 10, 1918, in France. Thomas H. Kirkpatrick, Jr., member of a quartermaster labor unit, succumbed to pneumonia. While most black soldiers served with transportation or labor units, Private Nathan Byrd, age twenty-three, of the Flea Hill community, was killed in action with the 367th Infantry Regiment, a unit of the Ninety-second Division, composed primarily of black enlisted men. The inscription on Byrd's tombstone in the Mount Zion AME Church graveyard speaks for all who did not come back from war: "Just in the morning of his days in youth and love he died."

Some Doughboys returned home wearing decorations for special bravery and service. Private Edward Draughton of the sanitary detachment of the Thirtieth Division won the new Distinguished Service Cross for bravery in action, as did First Lieutenant Daniel Byrd of Company F, 119th Infantry, the unit largely composed of Cumberland men. One who died of illness at the age of thirty in 1918, Captain Donald F. Ray of Fayetteville, nonetheless left a long-term legacy. As a lawyer on the staff of the Chief of Artillery in Washington, D.C., Ray pressed the case for his hometown as the site for an artillery range and training camp.

Death from illness at home, especially from influenza, was a major part of the war story. During the autumn and winter of 1918-1919, hundreds were sick and scores died, victims of an influenza pandemic that swept the country. Factory villages ran advertisements begging for medical help, and the pages of the newspapers were filled with obituaries, often of several members of a single family.

CHAPTER NINE

Between Two More Wars: 1920-1940

Fort Bragg and Pope Air Force Base

Cumberland County's twentieth-century destiny—to become home to one of the largest military bases in the world—began on a dusty June day in 1918 when a large white motorcar set out from Washington, D.C., headed south. In the car were Colonel E. P. King of the office of the chief of artillery, United States Army, and Dr. T. Wayland Vaughn of the United States Geological Survey. These men were under orders to reconnoiter a site for an artillery range and camp. For this trip, King and Vaughn found that there were few maps—and even fewer marked roads. "We traveled by the compass and dead reckoning," King later wrote. On the evening of their fourth day out of Washington, they topped a rise just beyond the crossroads of Manchester on the Lower Little River. King later recalled that as he and Vaughn looked out across the undulating, pine-covered sand ridges, they knew they had found the site they had been searching for. The War Department soon announced that "Camp Bragg" (named for Braxton Bragg, who had been a general in the Confederate States Army) would be located in the rolling North Carolina sandhills, as recommended by King and Vaughn.

A corps of carpenters and ditchdiggers—including hundreds of Puerto Rican and Haitian migrants—went to work carving roads, erecting hundreds of wooden buildings, and constructing

In 1918 the federal government authorized construction of Camp Bragg on a huge complex northwest of Fayetteville. In the photograph at top (January, 1919), an army of construction workers are lined up to receive payment for their labor. In the photo at bottom (March, 1919) is a nearly completed hanger at the installation. Photographs supplied by the author.

water and waste systems. When it was completed in the spring of 1919, the cantonment was capable of accommodating 16,000 soldiers. Meanwhile, an airfield for the "Flying Jenny" airplanes of a newfangled artillery-observation squadron had been laid down in a corner of the cantonment. In January, 1919, a young pilot, Lieutenant Harley Pope, and his companion, Sergeant W. W. Fleming, were killed when their plane crashed into the Cape Fear River just east of Fayetteville. The field was named to honor Pope.

World War I hostilities ended before construction of Camp Bragg was completed, but the army initially planned to keep the camp as a permanent home for artillery. About 1,200 troops were stationed there in 1919 and 1920. In the late summer of 1921, however, the War Department announced that the facility would be abandoned. Colonel Albert J. Bowley, the camp commander, sprang into action. He employed certain political connections and pressed the new secretary of war to visit and inspect the camp. He called on local boosters to spread a middle-of-the-day barbecue for the visitors. On September 14, 1921, the *Fayetteville Observer* issued a special edition with this giant headline: "CAMP BRAGG WINS."

Bowley remained commander of the camp he had saved until 1928. By then, the name had been changed to Fort Bragg and a 1923-1928 building program had replaced many of the canton-ment's original wooden structures with permanent brick buildings. Pope Field got a large hangar for its observation balloons. As early as July 4, 1923, soldiers were parachuting from balloon platforms, a harbinger of Fort Bragg's future role as "home of the Airborne." Additional construction in the 1930s created an installation of about 3,000 soldiers and 350 civilian workers. From the start, the post contributed significantly to the Cumberland economy. It spawned a fleet of "jitney" taxicabs linking the camp with the railroad depot in Fayetteville. Dozens of civilians became permanent employees in post laundries, kitchens, warehouses, offices, and public works.

Population Perspective

Between 1920 and 1940, population grew at the sharply increasing rate common throughout North Carolina. A diminishing infant mortality rate and modern medical practices resulted in unprecedented growth in a largely native population. From 1910

This view of Fayetteville's Hay Street, looking west, was made in the early 1920s. Note the streetcar track in the middle of the street. Photograph from Albert Y. Drummond (ed.), *Drummond's Pictorial Atlas of North Carolina* (Charlotte: Albert Y. Drummond, [1924]), 52.

to 1920 the combined population of Cumberland and Hoke counties (the latter was formed from the former in 1911) grew by 31 percent. Between 1920 and 1940 Cumberland's population surged by 70 percent—from 35,064 to 59,320. Black people accounted for a decreasing portion. They comprised 40.1 percent of the total county population in 1920 but only 34.5 percent in 1940. This pattern reflected differences between the races in the realm of mortality, as well as patterns of out-migration, particularly among the Depression-battered tenant farmers.

Fayetteville's population increased by 46 percent (from 8,887 to 13,039) between 1920 and 1930 and by 33.8 percent (from 13,039 to 17,428) between 1930 and 1940, with black people continuing to comprise a larger portion of the total population than in any other place of comparable size within North Carolina. Blacks represented 40 percent of the city's total population in 1940.

Culture

The post-World War I transformation of what is now called the American "life-style" changed Cumberland County considerably. The years were marked by the exploding popularity of automobiles, movies, and radio; by more liberal attitudes concerning sex; expanding horizons for women; and fast-paced improvements in medicine, living conditions, and education. In common with the nation, Cumberland experienced the exuberant optimism of the 1920s, the puzzled despair of the Great Depression, and the more sober and hopeful outlook spawned by the New Deal in the 1930s.

The county was a typical southern rural place, where church life continued to be important, even as public morals underwent change. Regional and statewide denominational groups met periodically in Fayetteville. Rural church reunions, camp meetings, and revivals abounded. Fayetteville's Roman Catholic congregation abandoned its 103-year-old church building on Bow Street in 1937 and moved into a handsome brick sanctuary in Haymount. A small group of black parishioners stayed behind, held their meetings in a barbershop, then founded St. Anne's on Ann Street in 1939.

The opposite end of the moral spectrum was symbolized by the headline in the *Fayetteville Observer* on July 13, 1921, which read: "Drive Immoral Women Out City, Officers Plan." The accompanying story revealed that General Bowley, commander at Camp Bragg, had met with Fayetteville's mayor and lawmen "to confer on women, liquor and speeding situation, and plans to end it all!" It was neither the first nor the last attempt to clean up the town. Such efforts may have succeeded for a season. But this headline of a few weeks earlier—"Immoral Women and Liquor are Easy to Secure"—could easily have been rerun. Such places as "Poe's Bottom" and "Blount Street" were notorious for prostitution and bootleg whiskey. In the 1930s "Sugar Hill" was a roadside district offering women, drink, and the "one-armed bandit"—the slot machine.

Between the poles of old-time religion and jazz-age vices, there were expanding social and civic activities. It was a time for joining. In Fayetteville the Parent-Teachers Association and the American Legion were organized in 1919, the Kiwanis Club and the YMCA in 1921 (there had been an attempt to organize a YMCA chapter as early as 1875 at Big Rockfish Presbyterian

Church), the Garden Club in 1925, the Chaminade Music Club in 1927, the Eastern Star in 1928, the Lions Club in 1933, and a chapter of the Daughters of the American Revolution in 1936.

Civic and patriotic celebrations continued to be important events, even during the Depression. In 1932, when Congressman Bayard Clark addressed the annual Confederate Memorial Day ceremony, the number of old soldiers had shrunk to nine from fourteen only a year earlier. In November, 1939, North Carolina governor Clyde Hoey and other dignitaries braved record low temperatures to participate in Fayetteville's outdoor commemoration of the 150th anniversary of North Carolina's ratification of the United States Constitution.

Modern sports increased in popularity. Textile factories had their own baseball teams. The 1921 Fayetteville High School football eleven won the state championship. A country club was built in 1921 (it paid deference to custom by observing a no-drinking rule on Sunday). Boxing cards at Fort Bragg drew large crowds, while the Sunday afternoon polo match on the post in the 1920s was a unique sporting event in the state. Women were increasingly seen on tennis courts and at swimming spots. Hunting and fishing continued to be popular recreations for the masses.

The dark side of society was expressed in the rigid racial segregation and sometimes violent racial animosity of the times. In 1921 a large advertisement proclaimed: "The Ku Klux Klan in Public Lecture at the Lafayette Theater. Ladies Especially Invited." Klan rallies and parades were reported periodically, although the organization lost favor in the 1930s. During the 1920s a flurry of vigilante action was spawned by the inability of lawmen to enforce Prohibition. A group known as "The Law and Order League of Grays Creek" operated briefly to battle illegal whiskey makers and dealers and to harass their customers. Improved law enforcement and the resumption of legal liquor sales in 1937 curbed trafficking in "woods whiskey," but bootlegging continued to be significant in the county's underground economy for another twenty years.

Politics

In politics this was the era of the "Solid South," and Cumberland County was a typical rock-ribbed Democratic place. The notable exception was the presidential election of 1928, during which Al Smith, the Roman Catholic from the sidewalks of New York, narrowly lost the county and the state to Republican Herbert Hoover. In Cumberland the vote was Hoover 3,534, Smith 3,297. Leading Democrats sat on their hands. But county party chairman Terry Lyons put together a full-page advertisement endorsing the ticket. It was signed by more than 150 women, including wives of the balking party stalwarts. The innovative campaign trick was indicative of the growing role of women as voters. In 1932 President Herbert Hoover, scarred by the Depression, lost the presidential election to Franklin D. Roosevelt; in Cumberland County the vote was Roosevelt 5,012, Hoover 931 (Socialist Norman Thomas garnered 40 votes). In 1936 it was FDR 6,505, Alf Landon 1,024.

In Democratic primary elections, Cumberland was usually in the camp of winning candidates for nominations for governor and United States senator. In 1936, however, the county supported a sometime favorite son, Dr. Ralph McDonald, over the eventual winner, Clyde R. Hoey. McDonald, the "insurgent" candidate, had been principal of Sunnyside School at Vander in the 1920s.

In local politics, action was confined to Democratic primaries for courthouse offices and the state legislature. The county was entitled to one seat in the state House of Representatives and, along with Bladen, Columbus, and Brunswick counties, which together comprised the state's Tenth Senatorial District, two seats in the state Senate. Most legislators served only a term or two. Most were lawyers, although W. C. Ewing, a businessman and political activist, served four terms, 1929-1937—three in the House and one in the Senate. Sheriff Hector McGeachy, first elected to that key courthouse office in 1910, served throughout the period. A leading political figure was Congressman Jerome Bayard Clark (1882-1959) of Fayetteville, a native of Bladen County and a lawyer-teacher who served ten terms in the United States House of Representatives, 1929-1949.

The Great Depression

The first blows of the Great Depression were felt in 1930-1931 as farm prices plunged, banks closed, mortgages were foreclosed, factories shut down, and local government paid employees in scrip. In 1933 volunteer relief efforts such as the PTA free-lunch program and an "Emergency Relief Canteen" were launched. By the following year the federal government's relief programs, known collectively as the New Deal, had come to Cumberland.

More than 120 projects totaling in excess of $300,000 and financed by the Emergency Relief Act and the Civil Works Act were carried out during 1934-1935. The largest of these was a $100,000 home sanitation project involving construction and installation of hundreds of wooden privies. (As late as 1940 only one in thirty farm homes in Cumberland County had indoor plumbing, and only one in nine had electricity.) Several miles of mosquito-control drainage ditches were dug in Fayetteville, Cedar Creek, Hope Mills, Flea Hill, and Wade. Roads were repaired, as were schools in Grays Creek, Eastover, Beaver Dam, Massey Hill, and Linden. Fayetteville Normal School got a playing field, a new road, and repairs—projects totaling $15,000. Salaries were provided for playground supervisors, cooks, nurses, secretaries, school lunchroom supervisors, workers for a "sewing room" program, a clerk for the "Transient Bureau," and a temporary photographer to take "before" and "after" pictures of repaired schoolhouses. The Fayetteville library became a free public facility for the entire county, and the first salary of a librarian, as well as an appropriation to repair books, came from Emergency Relief Administration funds. There were exotic projects such as $8,200 for "beautifying" the road between Fayetteville and Fort Bragg and $1,300 for a countywide effort at "propagating scuppernong grape vines." There were also humble projects such as emergency pasture for cattle that strayed from foreclosed farms, and seeds for home gardens.

The human face of the Depression was varied. Many people suffered economically; some "lost everything." Some remembered mostly the bewilderment and fear of uncertain times. But others who went through the lean years developed a tough pride in their survival. And there were those like the black woman who for an oral history project described the gardening and meat-preserving methods of the time. In her family, she said, "the suffering was not as great as [in] others. . . . [W]e had no money to lose[. W]e had been eatin' and we went on eatin'."

Government

The 1920-1940 period witnessed a steady enlargement of government's role in the lives of ordinary people. By 1920 many familiar local services were in place—public health, public welfare (1917), farm extension work (1914). During the 1930s the New Deal spawned a new array.

In 1931 the state took over the job of building and maintaining roads, previously the responsibility of North Carolina's individual counties. Fayetteville became the headquarters of a multicounty division of the State Highway Department and the State Highway Patrol. State assumption of road operations enabled Cumberland County to eliminate a local road tax of 12 cents on each $100 worth of valuated property. By the late 1930s major north-south and east-west highways were hard-surfaced, as was the road linking Fayetteville and Fort Bragg. Most rural roads in the county remained unpaved until after World War II.

The old-style 1909 bridge over the Cape Fear was replaced in 1937 by a modern concrete highway bridge, which was dedicated to men from the county who had served in World War I. In 1924 county government moved into a new courthouse on Gillespie Street in Fayetteville.

Fayetteville town government also expanded. The Works Progress Administration (WPA) financed a new armory (1936) for the Fayetteville Independent Light Infantry and a new city hall (1939) on Green Street. Street-paving projects were under way in every warm-weather season. The library of the Woman's Civic Association became a free public facility in 1932. Service was expanded into a countywide effort the following year. These services were for "white only," however; black people did not get a branch library until World War II.

Education

The 1920-1940 period witnessed steady improvement in public education, at least for white children. This was especially so after 1931, when the state took financial responsibility for teacher pay and operating expenses. A few years later the WPA provided money that spurred school construction. Hard times interrupted earlier improvements, with cuts in already meager teacher pay and, in 1931, a reduction in the length of Fayetteville's school term from nine to eight months. The ninth month was restored in 1936 when voters approved a local school tax of 15 cents per $100 valuation to supplement the state appropriations.

In Fayetteville the period opened with a successful school bond election in 1921. Otherwise disenfranchised black citizens were registered to vote in this election, and they voted unanimously in favor of the bonds. In fact, only three negative votes were counted. Alexander Graham (High) School was built, and Central was converted to an elementary school. A black high school was established in 1927 in the Orange Street building. In 1940, utilizing bond funds and WPA allocations, the city built a new Alexander Graham High School (Fayetteville High) and a new unit on Washington Drive for black E. E. Smith High School. The 1921 Graham school became a junior high. During this period the most noteworthy educational personalities in Fayetteville were two black men—Dr. E. E. Smith, whose fifty-year career as head of the normal school ended with his death in 1933, and Professor Edward Evans (1863-1943), a teacher and principal for fifty-four years.

In the county, the array of one-room schoolhouses and old-time academies began to give way to larger consolidated units for white children, which opened at South River (1921), Long Hill (1922), Linden (1922), Grays Creek (1922), Sunnyside or Vander (1924), Massey Hill (1925), Wade (1925), Godwin (1926), Stedman (1927), and Spring Lake (1938). By 1929 there were eight accredited high school programs with more than 350 graduates a year. Cumberland ranked eleventh among North Carolina's 100 counties in number of high-school graduates. Central High School (1938) absorbed the classes of four schools located east of the Cape Fear. By 1938 there were seven schools with high-school classes and nine other elementary schools for whites. Large elementary schools were Seventy-first, Eastover, and Cedar Creek.

For black children, the story was bleak. Not until 1939 did Armstrong School at present-day Eastover add classrooms and become the first high school for black students outside Fayetteville. It was named for its principal, Dr. E. A. Armstrong. At the time, there were forty-four schools for black children, with 126 teachers. Most of the schools were one- or two-room wooden buildings, many with poignantly lovely names such as Hickory Shade, Butter Branch, Lonely Hill, and Shaw Meadow. In 1911 Mrs. Ann Chesnutt Waddell (1888-1965) began a twenty-year tenure as "Jeanes supervisor" of black schools, an administrative post financed by northern philanthropy. In 1920 annual per-pupil spending for black children was $2.94, compared to $12.52 for whites. In 1940 the figures were $26.22 and $39.63 respectively.

During the 1920-1940 period there was but one school for Indians—Cades Hill just east of the Cape Fear from Fayetteville. Fort Bragg got its first school in 1922. Gladys Currie, who began teaching in 1923, was principal-teacher at this school from 1933 until her retirement in 1947. In the early 1920s a few schools hired buses with wooden bodies to transport children to classes, but not until 1934 did the county receive from the state its first familiar orange school buses.

Fayetteville's State Colored Normal School received increased state appropriations in the late 1920s as the demand for black schoolteachers grew. When Dr. E. E. Smith died in 1933, he was succeeded as president by Dr. J. W. Seabrook (1886-1974), who brought the skills of a professionally trained administrator to a post he would hold until 1956. Dr. Seabrook was influential in devising teacher-training standards for the state. Locally, he was an indefatigable champion of improved schooling for black children at a time of rigid racial segregation and inequalities in financial support. In retirement in the 1950s, he publicly hailed Supreme Court decisions outlawing segregation and called for integration of the schools. In 1937 the General Assembly designated the normal school as a four-year institution. In 1939 the name of the institution was officially changed to Fayetteville State Teachers College. Some of its graduates became the first wave of black teachers and administrators to preside over racially integrated schools and classrooms after World War II. When Dr. Seabrook retired, he was succeeded by Dr. Rudolph Jones, who got in hot water several years later by admitting that the school, always financially strapped, had often "graduated illiterates."

This wooden frame structure served as an early classroom building at Fayetteville's State Normal Colored School. The photograph was made in 1926. In 1939 the North Carolina General Assembly officially renamed the institution Fayetteville State Teachers College. Photograph from the files of the Division of Archives and History; reproduced courtesy Chesnutt Library, Fayetteville State University.

Health

Improvements in health were a phenomenon in the 1920-1940 period, although the most momentous revolution in the health field came after World War II. By the mid-1920s death rates for infants and adults were in uninterrupted decline. The disparity in the quality of medical care for blacks and whites endured. In 1925 three of four black babies were delivered by midwives, compared to 15.8 percent for white babies. Overall infant mortality was 61.6 deaths per 1,000 births.

The general health of the population during this period is told in statistics. In 1931 a pioneering check of schoolchildren found 31 percent of them with "bad teeth" and 30 percent with "defective tonsils." A decade later, when young men took Selective Service physicals, 42 percent of the white men and 60.8 percent of the black men were rejected—an overall rejection rate of just under 50 percent. Public health work grew, spurred by New Deal programs. In 1931 the county got its first black public health nurse, Elizabeth McMillan Thompson (1903-1982), whose no-nonsense skill with a needle became legendary among schoolchildren until her retirement in 1968.

Women

The period saw women moving into work and activities previously reserved for men. Teaching, nursing, operating telephone switchboards, and stenography became predominant fields of work for women. Female professionals also appeared. In 1920 Katherine Robinson, a pioneering graduate of the University of North Carolina Law School, joined her father, Henry McDiarmid Robinson, a former mayor of Fayetteville, in a hometown practice. Following her marriage to R. O. Everett, she moved to Durham. (In the 1980s she was still going strong and was being hailed as the nation's oldest practicing female attorney.) Dr. Jessie Ray Zachry, "very bright" holder of several advanced degrees, joined a local dentist in a brief partnership. In 1931 Lucille Hutaff, daughter of a Fayetteville soft-drink dealer, went off to medical school. During much of the 1920-1940 period Sallie W. Tomlinson was either town treasurer (1927) or town clerk (1933), the latter a post she held until 1950.

Black People

Despite rigid racial segregation and blatant racial discrimination, the 1920-1940 period was a time of growing achievement—and growing assertiveness—among Cumberland County's black people. It was also a time of increased mobility, of a steady migration of rural black people, as well as the sons and daughters of town families, to Washington, Baltimore, Philadelphia, and Chicago. By the 1940s Dr. Matthew Leary Perry, the son of a black builder-architect, could count thirty-four natives of Fayetteville who had become lawyers, doctors, pharmacists, or dentists—"a larger number than any other town in the state," he said.

Ties were especially strong between the county's black families and the District of Columbia. Scores of the South's black professionals received their training at two famous black institutions of higher learning—Howard University and Freedman's Hospital—located there. Drs. Edward Williston, John Sinclair Perry, and Howard Scurlock were heads of departments there. George Scurlock was a lawyer-businessman and political activist. All were natives of Fayetteville.

Of those who remained in Cumberland, a large majority were farmers. In 1920 nearly two thirds of the county's black farmers were tenants. Black workers were also heavily represented in the pine forests, as well as at sawmills, on riverboats, and in railroad yards. There were also black businessmen and professionals. In the 1920s, six black physicians and three dentists were practicing in Fayetteville. The most noted was Dr. Paul N. Melchor (1865-1928), an early graduate of Shaw University's medical school in Raleigh, who opened an office as early as 1897. Others included Melchor's son, Warren; Ben H. Henderson (1865-1928), also of Shaw, who began practice by 1909; F. D. Willison; A. L. Banks; and W. P. DeVane.

James T. Williston, one of North Carolina's early black druggists, operated a store on Person Street, and Harmon Perry had a drugstore on Gillespie Street. Their sons, Frank Williston and Dallas Perry, carried on the respective businesses. James McNeill (1840-1904) was the town's first embalmer; his son, Thomas Hall McNeill (1868-1933), and grandson, Thurman McNeill, carried on the family business on Bow Street. Dallas Perry was a builder-architect responsible for the construction of many residences, commercial buildings, and the soaring spire of

Hay Street (black) Presbyterian Church (1905), which was destroyed by fire in 1980. James Waddell was the town's leading brick-building contractor. Sam Drake and E. N. Williams were meat merchants. R. W. Thagard (1860-1928) operated a large grocery. Irving Carroll was a tailor and the proprietor of a "pressing club" (the 1920s name for a dry-cleaning establishment) on Market Square. Page Smith and Rosabelle Wright of Blounts Alley listed themselves as performers with "Kelly's Jazz Hounds," led by Walter Kelly.

Several black families were connected to the Sun Mutual Life Insurance Company, a local black-owned business. Most of the town's leading black families lived either on Moore or Gillespie Street, and most black businesses were located on Person or Gillespie Street. The descendants of antebellum wagoners and draymen became cab drivers or filling-station operators. In 1928 the residents of Mechanic Street, just off Moore, included a railroad worker, a plumber, a barber, a hairdresser, an employee of an ice plant, two bellhops, a tinsmith, a cook, a tailor, and a schoolteacher. The silk-fabric factory at the foot of "Ashley Heights" continued to be a significant employer of an all-black work force until it finally shut its doors just before World War II.

Churches, lodges, an all-black American Legion post, and the woefully inadequate schools of the day were institutional mainstays of black society. Participation in the political process was curtailed, although black professionals continued to vote and white politicians "sponsored" other black voters, especially in municipal elections. The New Deal spurred political activism. A branch of the National Association for the Advancement of Colored People was formed in Fayetteville in 1939.

The Economy

The economy went on a roller-coaster ride in the years between the world wars. There were good times and hard times, boom and bust. In the early 1920s "every cotton farmer wore a silk shirt," but in the depths of the Great Depression "you couldn't give cotton away." Farmers struggled with the unpredictable habits of prices, weather, and the boll weevil. The price of cotton, the major money crop, tells the story. It was $150 a bale in 1920, less than $70.00 in 1921, $100 in 1925, less than $55.00 in 1930, $13.00 in 1932, and $62.00 in 1936. Cotton income, about $3 million in 1925, dropped to $1 million in 1930 on a total crop smaller by one third. The price of tobacco, the other money crop, also fluctuated. The 1919 price of 47.4 cents a pound was a historic high. After that year, prices remained in the 20-cent range until the onset of the Depression, with a total annual crop valued between $600,000 and $700,000.

Behind the statistics was a way of life. A large majority of the county's farmers lived in a typical "shotgun" house set down next to the cotton fields. A cash crop of a few dozen bales brought a few hundred dollars annually. Water came from a pump or a well. Firewood from a nearby pine thicket was fuel for cookstove and fireplace. The diet was hog and hominy, with garden vegetables and melons in the summer. It was an age of mules and plows. In 1940 Cumberland had 2,900 farms and 4,500 farmers and farm workers, but only 120 tractors.

While farm prices moved up and down, prices of manufactured goods, especially cotton textiles and wood products, held steadier in the 1920s. Jobs were substantially secure—although still low paying—in the factories and mills. White workers predominated in the latter, except in the all-black silk factory in Fayetteville. Black workers predominated in lumbering operations and forest-product mills. The economy of the 1920s was up and down, but the 1930s brought a great bottoming—the Depression. Between 1930 and 1934 the price of cotton and tobacco plummeted to new lows, textile factories closed down, banks shut their doors, and sawmills fell silent. Total cotton income in 1932 was only $215,000 in the county. Tobacco brought 8 cents a pound.

The county emerged only slowly from the economic depths. Farm prices rose. Cotton went to $62.00 a bale in 1936 but slumped to $50.00 in 1937. Tobacco brought 24.3 cents a pound that year as the New Deal price support program took hold. In 1938 tobacco became the top money crop in Cumberland, bringing a total of $905,000, compared to $405,000 for cotton. Not until 1940 did employment recover to pre-Depression levels. In that year 20,000 people were wage earners—4,700 on farms, 3,500 in manufacturing, 10,300 in retailing and construction, and 1,500 on the expanding Fort Bragg payroll. In 1930, by comparison, there had been 6,000 paid workers on farms, 3,800 in manufacturing, and 7,800 in other jobs. Value added by manufacture, $2.7 million in pre-Depression 1927, was almost exactly the same in 1939.

The cotton factory villages of Hope Mills and Massey Hill were especially battered by the Depression. But families survived by planting gardens, fishing, raising chickens, and trading company scrip for groceries when cash had virtually disappeared. In 1934 a nationwide textile strike tested the sense of village togetherness fostered in the little houses clustered near the factories. For three weeks in September, strikers had mixed success in Cumberland. They forced the closure of one mill and then another. But they eventually were frustrated by nonstriking workers who crossed picket lines under the protection of National Guard troops from Parkton. When the national strike ended on September 22, all Fayetteville plants resumed operations.

There were few other examples of worker unrest, although in 1921, an earlier year of depressed prices, fifty to seventy-five "unskilled colored workers" at a Fayetteville woodworking plant made headlines when they walked off the job in a body after hearing that wages would be cut by 5 cents an hour. Their wages at the time ranged from $2.00 to $3.50 a day. In that same year, the town's seven-man police force—including two motorcycle cops—walked off the job after unsuccessfully demanding $100 a month in pay. The strikers were fired on the spot, and a new force was recruited in twelve hours from a pool of forty applicants.

Ownership of textile plants changed, with out-of-county firms buying from the founding owners. In Massey Hill, Burlington Mills acquired Puritan in 1929 and Faytex (Victory) in 1939. Tolar-Hart was sold to a Gastonia firm in 1941. Hope Mills plants were consolidated under the name Dixie-Mebane, later Dixie Yarns.

Trade

Cumberland shared in the diversification of retail enterprise as America entered the age of consumer goods. The automobile ushered in a new era of filling stations, garages, and sales lots, which were quickly followed by the "tourist court," which served the traveling public. The 1920s saw downtown Fayetteville's old merchandising district change to reflect new needs. Automobile dealerships, "electrical companies," and the "five and dime" sprang up beside the older mercantile, hardware, and farm-supply establishments. The mid-1920s witnessed a notable building boom. In 1925-1926 Highsmith-Rainey Hospital opened a modern new facility on Haymount. A new courthouse opened on Gillespie Street. The seven-story Prince Charles Hotel and the ten-story National Bank of Fayetteville went up at each end of Hay Street. In 1924 one of the first "suburban" subdivisions, Sherwood

In this view of the 400 block of Hay Street, Fayetteville, looking east, the seven-story Prince Charles Hotel, erected in the mid-1920s, dominates the skyline. Photograph (ca. 1930) supplied by the author.

Forest, was laid out between old plank-road routes in the Haymount section west of downtown Fayetteville.

New businesses served the new life-styles of the post-World War I era—the age of jazz, the motion picture, the radio, and the motorcar. By the 1930s Fayetteville had four movie houses. In 1927 health inspectors gave grades to 9 "cafes," 7 "restaurants," and 4 "wienie stands." In 1932 a rotogravure section of the *Fayetteville Observer* featured a firm that had defied the "sick world" of the Depression and was actually prospering. It was the Fayetteville Vending Machine Company, "the South's largest distributor for the world's leading manufacturers of coin operated devices." Jukeboxes, gaming machines, and penny scales were sold and serviced in a sales territory "extending from Maine to the Rio Grande." In 1939, 467 retail establishments in the county and 267 in Fayetteville employed 1,392 workers.

Transportation and Communications

In 1920 the mule cart and buggy were still important for personal transportation, the train and the river steamer for long-distance travel. But the motorcar was taking over. By 1927, when the state began financing hard-surfaced roads, 5,326 automobiles were registered in the county, and Fayetteville had two motorcycle policemen. The numerous mule corrals and sales barns familiar for fifty years disappeared from the town. By the early 1930s motoring tourists were passing through the county on numbered highways (although Fayetteville voters rejected a bond issue to finance a municipal advertising campaign to attract motorists). It was the heyday of the ornate auto service station. Hilltex Service Station opened on Haymount in 1924. Its "half-timbered style" building included seven pumps and seven "air stations." It had a "ladies rest room, with lounge and rocking chairs." Proprietor J. H. Haines described himself as "a regular automobile doctor." As "jitneys" and "cabs" replaced the horse-drawn "hacks," the taxicab business became important. Olen Gerald, Sr. (1892-1985), a black businessman, established Hillsboro Taxi Company in 1941. Its vehicles transported Fort Bragg servicemen for forty years.

Fayetteville continued to be a major railroad freight and passenger center. Travelers had a choice of more than thirty passenger trains a day, including the famous high-speed New York-to-Florida specials. Washington, Norfolk, and Philadelphia were only hours away by train. The Cape Fear River's days as a freight and passenger route came to an end by the early 1920s. The last of the river steamers, the *A. P. Hurt*, first placed in service during the Civil War, burned in Wilmington in 1923. In the early 1930s completion of a third lock on the lower river raised hopes of a new era of bulk traffic, especially in petroleum. Fayetteville financed a bulk terminal that—before its demise in the 1960s—was known as "the port of Fayetteville." Trucks and railroads killed off the bulk river trade soon after World War II. The river reverted to its ancient role as a haunt of fishermen, boaters, and wildlife enthusiasts.

In communications, the county's major newspaper, the *Fayetteville Observer*, became a modern-looking daily journal after 1923, when Charles Wilson began a twenty-five-year tenure as publisher-owner. The paper acquired new presses and other equipment and moved to larger quarters. The county got its first radio station, WFNC, in 1939.

World War II

In the summer of 1940, as headlines told of German armies sweeping through the Low Countries and France, census takers took the count in Cumberland County. They found 59,320 people (34.5 percent of whom were black), including 17,428 people (40 percent black) in Fayetteville. The army population at Fort Bragg and Pope Air Field was 5,000. Within a few months, events across the Atlantic would dramatically change the population figures—and the way of life—of Cumberland County.

As the United States mobilized against the threat of war, Fort Bragg was given a major role in the expansion of the army. In August, 1940, the post was designated the training site for the Ninth Infantry Division, for artillery replacements, for draftees, and for several engineer and service units, among them the "41st Engineer General Service Regiment (colored)," an all-black outfit nicknamed "the singing engineers." Thousands of young men poured in by train, bus, and auto. A temporary city of tents went up, and a furious barracks-construction program was launched. Soon, dusty country roads were jammed with columns of marching soldiers and armies of carpenters, plumbers, electricians, and other construction workers. Earlier than almost any place in the nation, Cumberland was transformed by preparations for war.

In nine months, 30,000 workers built 2,739 wooden barracks at a cost of $44 million. On October 22, 1940, the *Fayetteville Observer* reported that the post population had reached 18,758, surpassing that of Fayetteville. In June, 1941, *Life* magazine profiled Fort Bragg in twelve pages of pictures and text under the subtitle "With 67,000 men, It Is Army's Biggest Camp."

The roiling changes by turns thrilled, overwhelmed, and appalled the people of Cumberland. At Christmas, 1940, hundreds of families opened their homes and offered holiday cheer to soldiers stationed far from their own homes. Meanwhile, the army reported that for its mess hall holiday feasts it had laid in 12 tons of turkey, 4½ tons of "mixed nuts," and 300 pounds of candy. For some families, the holidays were saddened. A series of fatal accidents at crowded rural crossroads brought protests and demands for improvements to the dusty farm roads now throbbing with traffic. Fayetteville, overwhelmed by the influx of humanity and vehicles, hastily formed a volunteer police auxiliary to assist the hard-pressed force of a half-dozen officers.

By December, 1941, more than 90,000 troops crowded Bragg and Pope. When homes again opened for Christmas, the nation was at war. Thousands of the young men would soon be boarding trains to embark for war fronts.

Famous Military Units

Among the units that went off to war from Fort Bragg and gained fame in battle were the Ninth Infantry Division, which landed in North Africa in November, 1942, stormed across Utah Beach on D-Day, June 6, 1944, and fought in Belgium and Germany. On D-Day, the famous original airborne divisions—the 82nd and the 101st—parachuted behind enemy lines on Utah Beach. They fought in December, 1944, in the "Battle of the Bulge." The 82nd fought in Sicily in 1943. The 13th and 11th Airborne divisions were activated in 1943 at the new Airborne Training Center at nearby Camp Mackall and fought in Germany and the Pacific. The all-black 41st Engineer Group went overseas in 1942 and built airfields in Africa and Europe. The 13th Artillery Brigade fought in Italy. More than fifty artillery battalions formed at Fort Bragg scattered to every theater of the war. A unit that did not get overseas was the 555th Parachute Infantry Battalion, the army's only all-black airborne unit, which trained at Camp Mackall. It was sent to the Pacific Northwest, where its soldiers pioneered the "smoke-jumper" technique of fighting forest fires.

The Post

Hundreds of county people worked on the Fort Bragg post as stenographers, kitchen helpers, repair and maintenance workers, laundry workers, and in engineering crews. The attraction of government work drew thousands of new people to the county, with the result that by war's end the population was half again as large as it had been in 1940. Many of these people remained for a lifetime. Margie Mann, who started as a clerk-typist interviewing draftees in 1944, retired forty-one years later as a personnel specialist. Famous visitors came to the post, including President Franklin Roosevelt, British prime minister Winston Churchill, and entertainers such as Bob Hope. Thousands of draftees got their first taste of army life in the barracks and pinewoods. Their letters home made Fort Bragg familiar throughout the land. The life of the draftee was depicted in the best-selling book *See Here, Private Hargrove* (1942), by Charlotte newspaperman Marion Hargrove, who called himself "the epitome of the confused but happy civilian in uniform."

Before and during America's entry into World War II, Fort Bragg attracted a number of prominent visitors, foremost of whom was President Franklin D. Roosevelt, who visited Fayetteville in March, 1941. Pictured with the president (*left*) are (*left to right*) Hector Blackwell, mayor of Fayetteville; J. Melville Broughton, governor of North Carolina; and Major General Jacob Devers, commanding general, Ninth Infantry Division, Fort Bragg. Photograph supplied by the author.

One of the best descriptions of the post—and of the county—during the war years was penned by British historian Napier Crookenden. He wrote of the soldiers of the airborne divisions:

The men worked hard and would have liked to have played hard, but facilities for entertainment on the isolated post of Fort Bragg in the pines and sand of North Carolina were very limited. On Saturday nights, the nearby country town of Fayetteville heaved and rocked and every bar was packed. The main bar, the Pump, was often the scene of fights between parachute soldiers and glider troops, between men of the 82nd and men of the 101st, between the Airborne and the rest of the Army—and between everybody and the Military Police.

During World War II one of the most popular gathering places for servicemen was Fayetteville's Town Pump Bar. This photograph shows the Pump on a typical evening about 1945. Photograph supplied by the author.

The Home Front

The wartime experiences of those who stayed at home were typical of people throughout the nation. There were shortages and rationing. But farmers were pleased when prices for crops went up sharply. Hundreds of county men and women went off to good-paying war-industry jobs elsewhere. Women who stayed home

During World War II, women on the home front made noteworthy contributions to military efforts abroad by volunteering their time to perform public service work in a variety of endeavors. These Fayetteville women enrolled in a Red Cross class that taught them how to make bandages. Photograph supplied by the author.

joined in Red Cross "sewing bees" at the courthouse. They prepared "comfort packages" for shipment overseas. Families cultivated "victory gardens," salvaged tin cans, and accepted the rationing that allowed them three gallons of gasoline a week and a pound of sugar a month. In 1944 there was a drive for relief of an ally, under the slogan "Russia Needs Clothing." With a wealth of marching units available, there were "Infantry Day" parades and Fourth of July celebrations. In mid-1944 Highsmith-Rainey Hospital became one of the first such facilities in North Carolina to be authorized to use the new wonder drug penicillin, "now available for civilians."

While civilians coped with the exigencies of the times, off-duty soldiers could find a cup of coffee at the "Soldiers Rest" club in the former Methodist parsonage on Old Street. There were also USO clubs. And there was a proliferating array of beer joints, roadhouses, and houses of prostitution. To deal with a rising tide of venereal disease among troops who frequented brothels, the army established four off-post VD treatment clinics. A post guidebook for soldiers written by twenty-eight-year-old Lieutenant Temple Fielding, who would become a postwar writer-publisher of travel guides, urged soldiers to visit a clinic as soon as possible after visiting with prostitutes.

Off to War

Approximately 1,100 Cumberland County men were listed by the state Adjutant General's Office as soldiers or sailors in World War II. They included about 780 whites and 341 black men. About a dozen were killed or died of battle wounds. About fifty were wounded in battle. Another dozen died of illness.

Politics

Public life generally took a back seat to the war. Cumberland continued its strong Democratic tradition. Franklin D. Roosevelt carried the county over Wendell Wilkie in 1940 by a margin of 6,050 to 1,118 votes, and over Thomas E. Dewey in 1944 by 6,615 to 2,014. In the 1944 Democratic primary election for governor, voters were closely divided between R. Gregg Cherry, the victorious candidate of the dominant wing of the party, and insurgent Dr. Ralph McDonald, formerly the principal at Sunnyside School, who had carried Cumberland in 1936. This time Cherry received 2,789 votes, McDonald 2,294.

The Postwar Era

As World War II victory celebrations ended and Cumberland veterans flocked home from the battlefields, many may have expected a return to familiar prewar patterns—of quiet days in small towns, in cotton-factory villages, at country crossroads. If so, they were in for a surprise. First there was a natural event, a record-breaking flood. The rain-swollen Cape Fear surged out of its banks on September 21, 1945. Water swirled within a block of the Market House. Dozens of box cameras came out to take snapshots of rowboats on Person Street.

The water quickly receded. But the years following World War II turned out to be the fastest-changing times in the entire story of Cumberland. Three momentous trends marked the postwar years: (1) Exploding population growth turned the county from a rural and small-town place to a sprawling urban area, with the typical variety of work and life-styles common to postwar America; (2) the civil rights revolution transformed educational, political, and social institutions and habits, opening new horizons and new opportunities for black people; (3) economic diversification swept away the historical farm-and-textile-factory industrial base and replaced it with a mixed industrial, commercial, and home-construction economy, with the suburban shopping center as its most familiar expression.

Population Perspective

The county's population exploded after 1940. From 59,320 that year, it grew by 62 percent in the wartime decade, 55 percent more in the 1950s, and yet another 43 percent in the 1960s, reaching 212,000 in 1970. Growth slowed in the 1970s. The population was as stable as it had been in sixty years, still reaching 247,000 in 1980, at which time Cumberland had become North Carolina's fourth most populous county.

The percentage of the population represented by black people declined from 34.5 in 1940 to 23.9 in 1970, a historic low. The 1970s saw a dramatic increase, however, to 30.7 percent as the all-volunteer, unsegregated army attracted more young black men and women. Even more dramatic was the change from rural to urban. In 1940, 28.9 percent of the population lived in an urban setting; by 1960 this percentage had increased to 47.3. By 1980 the urban population had grown to nearly 80 percent. Suburban subdivisions and mobile-home parks marched across former cornfields, cotton rows, and pinewoods. In 1970 the United States Bureau of the Census announced that the "urbanized area" of the county was second only to Mecklenburg County in North Carolina.

Curbed by a quirk in state annexation laws, Fayetteville had trouble extending its boundaries to take in the burgeoning suburbs. Nonetheless, its population grew from 34,715 in 1950 to 60,000 in 1980. The former textile-factory town of Hope Mills, with fewer than 1,800 residents as late as 1970, grew into a residential community of more than 5,000 by 1980. Spring Lake experienced similar growth. In 1980 it was home for more than 6,000 people, mostly soldiers and airmen and their families.

Civil Rights

Of all the postwar changes, the most momentous was the civil rights revolution—the ending of legalized racial discrimination and the movement of black people into the mainstream of economic, educational, political, and social life. The changes that occurred in Cumberland were part of a national story. But Cumberland's story had unique features of its own as well.

The initial postwar years saw an uneasy return to prewar racial customs. Rigid racial segregation was still the order of the day. Change was coming, however, but slowly. Early signs were at Fort Bragg. In 1947 the all-black 555th Parachute Infantry Battalion was disbanded, its troops gradually absorbed into other units of the 82nd Airborne Division. In 1951 Mildred Poole, principal of the Fort Bragg post school system, took a pioneering step by ending racial segregation in the twenty classrooms under her authority. Her action has been called the earliest instance of integration on a federal installation in the South. In the same decade, Fayetteville and county school systems launched building programs that included some modern facilities for black children, many of whom were attending classes in one- or two-room schools built fifty years earlier. Fayetteville State Teachers College received additional state appropriations for dormitories, classrooms, and a library for its expanding all-black student body.

Segregation remained the rule, however. Despite the May, 1954, decision by the Supreme Court of the United States declaring classroom segregation unconstitutional, Mildred Poole's racially mixed classes remained unique. A black army officer described the existing situation in these words: "Blacks were restricted to the balcony of the local theater and rode at the back of the bus to and from town. And when we protested such bigoted practices, we were the ones who were disciplined. The families of black troops at Fort Bragg lived in converted army barracks in a segregated area called Spring Lake, but which General [Jim] Gavin [82d Airborne Division commander] called a 'mud puddle.'" Blacks were not served in most of the restaurants and beer parlors in Fayetteville. Separate waiting rooms were maintained in the train depot, the bus station, the county health department, and the hospital.

The situation grew increasingly intolerable, as explained years later by Dr. Charles "A" Lyons, Jr., by then president of Fayetteville State University. Lyons, a veteran of the Korean War, said: "I went over to fight for democracy. I came home to enjoy that democracy, and had a rude awakening. I was thrown out of a sandwich shop in my hometown of Tarboro while still wearing my uniform."

Fayetteville's small but active black middle class had some political success in 1949 when Dr. W. P. DeVane was elected to the city council. He was defeated four years later. Fred Burns, a teacher and barber, had broken the ice for DeVane by running unsuccessfully for the city council in 1947 as the first black man to offer himself as a candidate for public office in Cumberland in more than a half-century. The council followed the lead of other communities by naming some black men as police officers—Josh Council, Joe Campbell, Calvin Bennett, Fred Lonnie Truitt, and Albert Algie Banks. These were largely token accommodations, however.

The far-reaching break, the new direction, came with dramatic suddenness in February, 1960. On the morning of February 10, "30 or 40" young black people, "presumed to be students at Fayetteville Teachers College," quietly "sat in" at the lunch counters in two Fayetteville stores. They were joining in a movement that had begun on February 1 in Greensboro and ultimately would receive national attention and transform the civil rights revolution. The eating facilities were promptly closed, then reopened. A week later, the students were back, this time walking the sidewalks as placard-carrying pickets. Young men and women from an institution that had begun as a school for freed slaves were writing a new chapter in the drive for equality.

In 1962 growing numbers of students picketed and sat in at restaurants and theaters. In June, 1963, they were joined by adults—and by soldiers, black and white, from Fort Bragg. Police fired tear gas to break up street demonstrations. Members of the local chapter of the NAACP, black ministers, teachers, physicians, mothers and fathers, and businessmen attended rallies and

Civil rights demonstrations by blacks were occasional occurrences in Fayetteville in the 1960s, as they were throughout the nation. In 1963 these students at Fayetteville State Teachers College picketed a downtown Fayetteville department store, urging citizens not to patronize the store because of its hiring practices. Photograph courtesy Fayetteville Publishing Company; supplied by the author.

donated money for bail. The *Fayetteville Observer* later rated these events as the "top story of 1963."

By autumn of that year a biracial committee had been formed and the first steps were being taken to dismantle segregation. They were often timid and grudging steps. But they were the beginning, and there would be no turning back. Signs pertaining to race came down at the health department and in the dining room of the hospital. The city pledged to hire blacks to fill public posts. Two black men became deputy sheriffs, "the first in Cumberland history." Some theaters and restaurants opened seats and counters (six Hay Street facilities continued to resist, however, some until the federal Civil Rights Act of 1964 became law). Fayetteville State Teachers College got its first white student, a schoolteacher taking remedial courses.

Racial integration in the public schools went into effect in the autumn of 1962 when four black children were assigned to all-white schools in Fayetteville. "Mixing Done Without Fuss," trumpeted a newspaper headline. In 1963 a total of sixty black children had crossed the line in city and county schools. In 1965 the number grew to 324 in the county and 86 in the city. That year, young Dr. C. R. Edwards, pastor of the First Baptist Church, became the first black man in modern times to serve on the Fayetteville board of education. Full-scale integration of the county's schools took place in the early 1970s.

Fort Bragg and Pope Air Force Base

Following World War II Fort Bragg and Pope Air Force Base remained large places, the permanent home of the 18th Airborne Corps and the 82nd Airborne Division, First Support Command; the Green Berets or Special Forces; and the 317th Tactical Airlift Wing—all major military units. The military population grew from a 1947 postwar low of 17,000 to more than 40,000 in 1951 during the Korean War. It has remained at that level for more than thirty years. Troops from Fort Bragg served in Korea, in the Dominican Republic in 1965, in Vietnam beginning in 1964, in Grenada in 1983. Museums and memorials on the post tell of the exploits of these troops and honor those who died. Eighty-four men with Cumberland addresses were listed as killed in action in the war in southeast Asia, 1964-1973, among them Abraham Lincoln Fields and Robert Lee Henderson, both of Spring Lake.

The appearance of the post changed. Hundreds of wooden wartime barracks were replaced by dormitory-type structures. A new hospital, new schools, and new housing areas for families were built. By 1980 more than a half-billion dollars had been spent on postwar construction at Fort Bragg and Pope. The military payroll grew to more than a billion dollars annually. In addition to those in uniform, more than 7,000 civilians were on military payrolls.

Increased pay and a peacetime environment encouraged stability. By 1980 more than half the uniformed men and women resided with their families. The 45,000 soldiers and airmen in uniform had nearly 70,000 "dependents," including 4,300 children in post schools. Another 15,000 children were in civilian schools, about a third of the total school population. More than half the personnel lived off-post in civilian-style housing. The demographics of military personnel changed as well, with increasing numbers of black and Hispanic soldiers and airmen. Women comprised nearly 10 percent of the total force. Several thousand military people continued to live in the community as retirees. Many took up second careers, especially in real estate, government, and health services. The big Veterans Medical Center, opened just before World War II, served thousands of retirees and other veterans.

Public Affairs

After World War II local government scrambled to keep up with the galloping horses of population growth and economic expansion, replacing its leisurely county-courthouse pace with a high-speed metropolitan one. The immediate postwar years witnessed an unprecedented array of civic projects. Fayetteville Municipal Airport, known as Grannis Field, opened in 1949 as a dirt-runway facility. Piedmont Airlines immediately inaugurated service there. Twenty years later, runways were surfaced and a modernistic terminal was built. Fayetteville was the recipient of a new central fire station (1949), a new Cape Fear Valley Hospital (1952), and two new libraries.

New roads built to cope with postwar traffic altered commercial patterns. Four-lane Bragg Boulevard, completed during World War II, linked city with post. The four-mile-long road quickly became a commercial artery lined with shopping centers, businesses, and outdoor theaters. In the early 1950s a new bridge over Cross Creek and a four-lane U.S. Highway 301 diverted tourist and truck traffic away from the Market House downtown. The state "Good Roads" program provided the funds to blacktop several hundred miles of rural roads, and state and local appropriations did the same for town and city streets.

In the 1950s Fayetteville adopted the city-manager plan of government, inaugurated a parks and recreation program, and cooperated in public housing programs by replacing hundreds of wooden cottages, mostly in black neighborhoods, with cinder-block and brick "projects." The 1960s and 1970s saw more such efforts, partially financed by new state and federal programs. Cape Fear Valley Hospital added mental-health and physical-rehabilitation wings. Fledgling physicians trained at the Fayetteville Area Health Education Center. An enlarged airport terminal, a 6,000-seat civic auditorium, a large new public health facility, and a modernistic courthouse and law enforcement center replaced older structures.

In the 1970s additional highway projects were completed. An unfinished gap in Interstate 95 was plugged east of the Cape Fear. An "all American Freeway" linked Fort Bragg to the metro area. A bypass swept around the urban area, providing sites for large shopping centers and residential developments. A second bridge crossed the Cape Fear. A partially completed "downtown business loop" threatened to obliterate the site of the Fayetteville Arsenal. During the 1973 oil crisis, the state even financed an eight-mile experimental commuter bicycle trail along the bypass. A "down-town circulation plan" was devised, and elaborate revitalization schemes were drawn, even as downtown lost its historic merchandising role. The Public Works Commission built multimillion-dollar regional sewer systems and two big riverside water-treatment plants. It began producing "peak load" electric power.

Politics

Democrats continued to dominate local and state politics throughout the postwar period. In local elections, Republicans offered only token opposition; contests were decided in Democratic primary elections. Population growth and "one man, one vote" judicial decrees enhanced the county's representation in the state legislature. By 1970 the county was entitled to five of the 120 seats in the state House of Representatives and two of the fifty seats in the state Senate. Voters tended to return willing incumbents for as many two-year terms as they sought. John Henley, a Hope Mills pharmacist, served twenty years in the House and Senate. Lura Tally, an educationist, was the first woman from the county to be elected to the state legislature (1972); she continued to serve in the state Senate sixteen years later. Among county legislators associated with major issues was state Representative Sneed High, who in 1961 led an unsuccessful effort to abolish the death penalty.

The growing strength of black voters was demonstrated in 1982 when two black men—Dr. C. R. Edwards and Nick Jeralds—were elected to the legislature and a black woman— Mary McAllister—was elected a county commissioner. The Reverend Aaron Johnson, formerly a Fayetteville city councilman and civil rights leader, was appointed head of the state prison system in the cabinet of Republican governor James G. Martin in 1985.

In municipal politics, businesswoman Beth Finch was elected Fayetteville's first female mayor in 1975. In 1981 Virginia Thompson Oliver became the first woman to head the Cumberland County Board of Commissioners and later was the first woman to head the North Carolina Association of County Commissioners.

In the early postwar years, urban-rural battles were fought over spending for schools, hospitals, and recreational facilities. Later, county government became increasingly progressive as its budget was larded with federal and state appropriations. By 1980 it had a professional county manager, a health department with more than 100 employees, a department of social services with 350 employees, and a public library system with a half-dozen facilities. On its payroll was a full-time archaeologist charged with researching historic sites and structures, as well as an adviser on computers. Workaday political influence was centered in the sheriff's office, in a coterie of politically active lawyers, and, until the 1970s, in rural volunteer fire departments. Black churches, civic organizations, and schoolteacher groups also wielded considerable influence and provided precinct workers.

Among political personalities, Cumberland claimed the state's governor, 1961-1965, Terry Sanford (b. 1918), a native of Scotland County and a veteran of World War II, who was practicing law in Fayetteville when elected in 1960. Twenty-six years later, Sanford brought his 1986 campaign for the United States Senate to the grounds of a Fayetteville high school named in his honor. The following day, he won the election. Charles G. Rose III of Fayetteville, whose father and grandfather were longtime political leaders, was elected to the United States House of Representatives in 1972 at the age of thirty-three and reelected eight times through 1988. In primary elections to choose Democratic candidates for governor, county voters supported the eventual winner—sometimes narrowly—in every election from 1948 to 1980. Democratic candidates easily carried the county in general elections.

In presidential politics, voters were for winners Harry Truman in 1948, John F. Kennedy in 1960, and Lyndon B. Johnson in 1964. In 1948, however, States' Rights party candidate Strom Thurmond received 25 percent of Cumberland's vote, the first sign that white voters were slipping their one-party moorings. In 1968, with the civil rights revolution in full swing and black voters participating in significant numbers, Cumberland divided almost evenly among Democrat Hubert Humphrey, segregationist George C. Wallace's American party, and Richard Nixon, the Republican and ultimate winner. Humphrey received a small plurality of a record total vote of more than 28,000, a 50 percent increase over that of 1960.

In 1972 Nixon overwhelmed Democrat George McGovern in the county as elsewhere. In 1976 the increasingly volatile electorate turned again. Democrat Jimmy Carter of Georgia was a big favorite over Republican President Gerald R. Ford. The total vote climbed to more than 38,000. President Carter, who visited Fayetteville for the wedding of his niece in 1979, led Ronald Reagan in Cumberland by a small margin in the 1980 election. The people of Cumberland seldom played roles in national politics, although in 1972 educator Jeanette Melvin Council of Fayetteville was the first black woman from North Carolina to serve as a delegate to a Democratic National Convention.

Economic Growth

In the early postwar years the economy remained grounded in its prewar elements: farming, main-street merchandising, and a cotton textile industry with historic roots—all leavened by the enlarged military payroll. Most textile workers labored in factories familiar for generations in Hope Mills, Massey Hill, and downtown Fayetteville. But most plants were now owned by large firms such as Burlington Mills or Dixie Yarns. The paternalistic mill-village society was disappearing as blacks and commuters obtained jobs in the plants. Several postwar years were good for textiles. By

1965, however, fewer than 4,000 workers were in manufacturing, barely an eighth of the work force. In 1970 only 3,000 were in textiles, and the decline was to continue.

Meanwhile, a new wave of industrialization began. The county joined the lively competition of southern places fishing for industry migrating from northern states. Between 1967 and 1973 Cumberland landed a half-dozen major national firms. The first was Rohm and Haas, a Philadelphia-based manufacturer of polyester (its big plant east of Fayetteville was later purchased by Monsanto Corporation). Next was Black and Decker (1967), followed by Purolator (1968) and Kelly-Springfield (1968), a subsidiary of the Goodyear Tire and Rubber Company. By 1980 Kelly-Springfield was the largest private employer in the county, with 2,600 workers in its large plant on Raleigh Road. In 1970 E. I. du Pont de Nemours opened a large plastics plant on the Cape Fear River at the Bladen line. The era of big-company migration waned, but not before Western Publishing Company, a national producer of games, comic books, cookbooks, and books for children, built a regional assembly center (1973) and Westinghouse Corporation erected a meter-manufacturing facility (1980).

In 1972 these additions, plus expanded local industries such as Fasco, Inc., a maker of cooling equipment, sent manufacturing employment to a postwar peak of just over 12,000 people—one fifth of the work force. By that year, textiles were fading even faster. Burlington Industries (formerly Burlington Mills) began to close local plants. Puritan and Lakedale, the old names, soon were gone. Smaller firms moved in, often remaining for but a brief time. By 1980 only 2,300 of 11,000 manufacturing workers were employed in the textile industry.

Commercial Growth

Merchandising—the buying and selling that was as old as John Newberry's gristmill on Cross Creek—took on new dimensions after World War II. The county's first postwar shopping center opened on Bragg Boulevard in 1955. Known as Eutaw for a nearby Indian spring, it was soon followed by Bordeaux, in a neighborhood that once had been a country vineyard. By the 1970s dozens of medium-sized and small centers were scattered throughout the county. Ribbons of commercial growth spread along the expanding network of commuter streets and highways.

Retail sales, $44 million in 1948, exceeded $200 million in 1964 and reached a half-billion dollars in 1972. By then, suburban shopping centers claimed a larger share of retail sales than the historically dominant downtown district of Fayetteville. The pace quickened further in 1976 with the opening of Cross Creek Mall. This big regional shopping center, built on a former soybean farm four miles west of the Market House, quickly became the centerpiece of a veritable city-within-a-city of smaller centers and commercial strips. Major retailers moved overnight from downtown to the mall. In 1980 the Census Bureau rated Cross Creek Mall the largest single commercial site in North Carolina on the basis of total sales. Retail sales in the county exceeded a billion dollars in 1980. By then, 38,000 people were on the payrolls of more than 6,000 commercial enterprises.

Beginning in the 1960s, banking also expanded. By 1980 every major banking chain in the state was represented, several with handsome downtown headquarters buildings. Like other North Carolina metropolitan areas, the county voted in 1979 to

The sprawling retailing complex comprised by (*top to bottom*) the Westwood Shopping Center, Cross Creek Mall, and Cross Creek Plaza came into being in the 1980s and quickly dominated Fayetteville's commercial life. Photograph (1989) by Cramer Gallimore, Fayetteville Publishing Company; supplied by the author.

allow bar sales of cocktails. Nightclubs and bars associated with restaurants proliferated. Several large beer distributorships were major elements in the county's modest wholesale economy.

The Disappearing Farm

In 1945 farming was still the county's chief economic activity. Tobacco—spurred by wartime demand and high prices—had surpassed cotton as the leading cash crop. Fayetteville got its first postwar tobacco sales warehouse in 1946. In the 1960s, however, Cumberland experienced a trend familiar throughout the South: a massive migration from the farm. In 1940, 22,000 people—one third of the population—resided on farms. In 1950 there were 15,000. In the 1960s the number declined by 63 percent to fewer than 3,700, or only 1.7 percent of the total population. In 1980 there were but 614 farms, and fewer than 2,100 people lived on them.

Dwindling farm population was accompanied by a revolution in what was produced. After World War II 15,000 acres were planted in cotton and 5,000 acres were planted in tobacco. By 1980 cotton plantings had declined to only 1,400 acres. The tobacco market was no more. Soybean acreage more than doubled to 45,000. Annual farm sales were in the $40-$50 million range. A measure of the economic transformation was the fact that wages of the 6,000 workers in restaurants, fast-food outlets, and snack shops totaled twice the income from farm products.

Although many pine forests fell before the march of urban growth, woodland products provided significant income into the 1980s, much of it going to out-of-state lumber and pulpwood firms, owners of the larger tracts. In 1980 a single small chemical-products distributor included the word "turpentine" in its company name, the last reminder of a historic sector of the county's economy.

Housing

A growing population spawned a big housing industry, and real-estate sales became a major postwar service industry. Before there was plenty, however, there was shortage, especially between 1945 and 1965. Thousands of people lived in delapidated prewar or wartime cottages or crowded into mobile-home parks. As late as

1962 there were 871 backyard privies inside Fayetteville's city limits.

The late 1960s and 1970s saw an unprecedented boom in modern housing. By 1980 the stock of housing was increasingly new, and two thirds of the structures were less than twenty years old. More than 98 percent had full plumbing. One person in nine resided in a mobile home, but frequently more by choice than necessity. Modern apartment complexes, complete with swimming pools, tennis courts, and clubhouses, were increasingly popular. A luxury retirement apartment building and a townhouse complex went up in downtown Fayetteville near the new library, museum, and hospital.

Education

No postwar institution went through more change than the public schools. Population growth pushed enrollments to record levels almost every year in the 1950s and 1960s, threatening to overwhelm facilities and teachers. In the 1950s city and county systems launched building programs that replaced prewar build-ings—including many old wooden structures—with typical low-slung postwar schools. Federal dollars and racial desegregation spurred building programs. By the mid-1970s enrollments stabilized and pupil performance on state and federal tests equaled and even surpassed state and national averages. In 1985 county and city units were merged into the third-largest system in the state, with more than 46,000 pupils. Cumberland athletic teams won state championships, and a Fayetteville teacher—Ruby Murchison—was honored at the White House after being chosen national "Teacher of the Year" in 1976.

Beginning the postwar years as Fayetteville State Teachers College, the former school for freed slaves was reconstituted Fayetteville State University in 1973 and given the mission of becoming a full-service regional university. In 1980 it had 2,000 students in undergraduate and graduate programs. In the 1960s the new Fayetteville Technical Institute quickly grew to become one of the largest in North Carolina's system of vocational training institutions, with more than 5,000 full-time and part-time students. In 1987 it was renamed Fayetteville Technical Com-munity College. Methodist College opened in Fayetteville in 1960 with 82 students and grew to more than 500 by 1980.

Culture

In the postwar years the county got its own Fayetteville Symphony (1957), Fayetteville Little Theater (1962), and Fayetteville Museum of Art (1971). By 1980 there were ten radio stations and two independent television stations. The *Fayetteville Times*, a morning daily founded in 1973, joined the *Observer* as a regional newspaper. In 1950 John A. Oates, a longtime leader in the field of education, published *The Story of Fayetteville*, an 868-page collection of local-history materials. The county historical foundation published early colonial records. Historical restoration and preservation saved several significant antebellum structures. The state of North Carolina established a regional museum of history in Fayetteville. A "humanist-in-residence" project and a Fayetteville/Cumberland Arts Council promoted the arts in the 1970s.

Churches

The strong religious tradition continued in the postwar years. By 1970 there were more than 300 congregations, including approximately 110 Baptist, 50 Pentecostal Holiness, 40 Methodist, 27 Presbyterian, and 30 nondenominational. The largest individual congregations were Snyder Memorial (Southern Baptist), Saint Patrick's (Roman Catholic), and Northwood Temple (Pentecostal Holiness), with more than 2,000 members each. Among large predominantly black congregations were First Baptist of Fayetteville, Mount Sinai Baptist, Williams Chapel (Free Will Baptist), and Evans Metropolitan AME Zion.

Life-style and Images

Cumberland County experienced all the colorful changes in life-style common to postwar America, with some local singularities. As early as 1950 three entrepreneurs were convicted of displaying "indecent films" in Fayetteville. In the 1960s and 1970s Fayetteville gained a reputation as a "sin city," with drugs, pornography, and prostitution as major problems. The sensational Jeffrey MacDonald murder case (1970-1979), in which a young army doctor was tried for the murder of his wife and two small daughters in their Fort Bragg quarters, attracted national attention.

Efforts to overcome the negative image united civic leaders and government officials. In the 1980s, efforts began to pay off.

The notorious 500 block of Hay Street, in which bare-breasted dancers had entertained in a neon-lit array of beer parlors during the 1970s, was demolished. A new hospital and a pedestrian mall rose in its place. The Cumberland Community Foundation was launched in 1984 with a donation in the amount of $500,000 from Dr. Lucille Hutaff (1912-1987), a Fayetteville native who was the first woman to serve as a full professor at the Bowman Gray School of Medicine in Winston-Salem. A philanthropic trust established in 1961 from the estate of former nurse Florence P. Rogers increased in value to $4.5 million by the 1980s and was supporting artistic, educational, and child-welfare projects. In 1985 Fayetteville was designated a national "All America City" in recognition of a variety of betterment projects, particularly a successful drive to build a modern central library.

The county continued to face major problems, however. While many had come to enjoy both economic plenty and social satisfaction, a significant portion of the citizenry had yet to share fully in the prosperity or the power. Among the Cumberland population, rates of teen-age pregnancy, drug use, poverty, and violent crime were higher than the state average. There was apathy and resistance to some change. Voters rejected bond issues for expanding parks and recreational facilities.

Epilogue

As they prepared to enter the final decade of the twentieth century, the people of Cumberland County found themselves very much in the mainstream of modern American life. While coping with the challenges offered by fast-paced change in many aspects of their lives, they faced the future with optimism tempered by the realization that additional challenges could be expected.

The strong presence of the multibillion-dollar military complexes at Fort Bragg and Pope Air Force Base sustained the county economically. But a noticeable slowdown in the civilian economy prompted new efforts to expand job opportunities and attract new investment. The county's governmental services, particularly in the realms of education, public welfare, and health care, faced increasing demands from the public but also experienced declining financial support from both federal and state treasuries. Despite changed attitudes on the subject of race and expanded cultural resources, the county still found itself searching for ways to build more confidence and respect between black citizens and white citizens and for still wider opportunities for the appreciation of cultural values.

As the 1990s began, even the stability embodied in the military presence was at least brought into question by upheavals in places far from the Cape Fear River. Revolutionary democratic change swept the Soviet Union and eastern Europe, seemingly bringing to an end the superpower "Cold War" that for nearly forty-five years had mandated a national dependency upon vast military resources. Few historical scenes have been more symbolic than the autumn, 1989, visit by the defense minister of the Soviet Union to Fort Bragg. After chatting with American soldiers in the field, the Soviet commander sat down to an evening barbecue and

In a symbolic display of reduced East-West tensions, Soviet defense minister Dmitri Yazor visited Fort Bragg in October, 1989, and walked among members of the 82nd Artillery in the fort's Sicily Drop Zone. Photograph by Ken Cooke, Fayetteville Publishing Company; supplied by the author.

hoedown hosted by high-ranking officers of American airborne units and ended the memorable occasion with a solemn toast to peace and comradeship between the two nations and their armed services.

With such momentous changes occurring almost daily, it was no wonder that to many citizens the history of Cumberland County in earlier times was more a quaint tale than a living past to which they could relate. Nevertheless, there was a growing interest in and appreciation for the heritage of sturdy colonial settlers, of indomitable black people rising from under the burdens of slavery, of recurring growth and stagnation, of war and depression, of turn-of-the-century small-town peaceableness, and the turmoil of the civil rights revolution of the 1960s. Even in a place so transformed by more recent events, the past was very much prologue to present and future. An understanding of the heritage of the past was required to comprehend fully that present and that future. To know the past and to build upon that heritage was yet another challenge for the people of Cumberland County as the twenty-first century approached.

Bibliographic Essay

Official county and state records pertaining to Cumberland County are abundant and, except for occasional minor lacunae, cover the entire history of the county from its founding. The North Carolina State Archives in Raleigh, the offices of the register of deeds and the clerk of court in the county courthouse in Fayetteville, and the Cumberland County Central Public Library have originals or microfilm copies of deeds, minutes of the court of pleas and quarter sessions, minutes of the county commission, marriage bonds, tax lists, probate records, will books, estate accounts, and other official materials pertaining to education, transportation, the military, finances, and other subjects. Important new information concerning the Scottish settlement of Cumberland County is being uncovered by the Scottish Records Project, underwritten by the Carolina Charter Corporation. Microfilm copies of original records from Scotland are being deposited in the North Carolina State Archives.

Published primary materials include William C. Fields (ed.), *Abstracts of Minutes of the Court of Pleas and Quarter Sessions of Cumberland County,* October, 1755-January, 1791 ([Fayetteville]: Cumberland County Bicentennial Commission, 2 volumes, 1978); and Kate James Lepine and Anna Sherman (eds.), *Abstracts of Wills, Cumberland County, North Carolina, 1754-1863* (Fayetteville: Katana Co., 1984).

There are many entries for Cumberland County and its people in William L. Saunders (ed.), *The Colonial Records of North Carolina* (Raleigh: State of North Carolina, 10 volumes, 1886-1890); Mattie Erma Edwards Parker and others (eds.), *The Colonial Records of North Carolina, Second Series* (Raleigh: Division of Archives and History, North Carolina Department of Cultural Resources, projected multivolume series, 1963—); and Walter Clark (ed.), *The State Records of North Carolina* (Winston and Goldsboro: State of North Carolina, 16 volumes, numbered XI-XXVI, 1895-1906). Several key items for the colonial period are in William S. Powell (ed.), *The Correspondence of William Tryon and Other Selected Papers,* Volume I: *1758-1767* (Raleigh: Division of Archives and History, North Carolina Department of Cultural Resources, 1980).

Newspapers are a key source for Cumberland County history. A microfilm collection of all known copies of extant Cumberland County newspapers published from 1789 to the present is available at Cumberland County Central Public Library in Fayetteville. Commercially produced abstracts of eighteenth-century newspapers published in Wilmington, New Bern, and Edenton contain many Cumberland references. Abstracts of death and marriage notices from early nineteenth-century Raleigh newspapers are also helpful. The Fayetteville Publishing Company, publisher of the *Fayetteville Observer* and the *Fayetteville Times*, has issued indexes of the *Observer* for the periods 1913-1919, 1947-1954, and 1960-1963.

Archival collections in North Carolina house manuscript collections of Cumberland material. A sampling includes the Tillinghast Family Papers, the Larkin Newby Papers, and the Robert Preston Harriss Papers in the Manuscript Department of the William R. Perkins Library, Duke University, Durham; the Edward Joseph Hale Papers and the James Cochran Dobbin Letters in the Southern Historical Collection, University of North Carolina Library, Chapel Hill; and the Colin Shaw Papers and the John Hogg Company and John Huske and Company Account Books in the North Carolina State Archives. The latter also contains ledgers and other commercial materials from nineteenth-and early twentieth-century textile and mercantile firms in Cumberland. Of special interest are the Tolar, Hart, and Holt Mills Village Scrapbooks (1916-1924), compiled by Ollie Vick Livingstone and Lucy Currie, employees of the textile-manufacturing firms of that name. The Ollie Vick Livingstone Journal is in the possession of the Historic Fayetteville Foundation, Inc.

The North Carolina Collection, University of North Carolina Library, Chapel Hill, contains several printed guides and commercial directories published in Cumberland during the late nineteenth and early twentieth centuries, as well as voluminous later twentieth-century material published by local and state government agencies.

Other sources of statistical, educational, commercial, and related information include federal censuses; maps published by insurance companies; commercial directories, especially the valuable *Branson's*; surveys (typescript) of historic structures; archival materials in the Charles Chesnutt Library at Fayetteville State University; and various yearbooks published for United States Army units headquartered at Fort Bragg.

For information on prehistoric Cumberland County, there is the "Archeological Survey of Selected Portions in Cumberland County, North Carolina," by Kenneth W. Robinson (mimeograph publication by the Cumberland County Planning Board, 1986). Material on the county's Civil War history is available in published standard histories and rosters of North Carolina regiments, in general histories, biographies, autobiographies, diaries, and journals pertaining to General William T. Sherman's march through the county. For the history of the Fayetteville Arsenal, there is "The North Carolina Arsenal, Fayetteville, North Carolina: Historical and Salvage Archaeological Study" (a research report by Contract Archaeology, Inc., Alexandria, Virginia,

1973). For the home front, the "Diary of Melinda Ray, 1861-65" (typescript in the possession of the Historic Fayetteville Foundation, Inc.) is a unique eyewitness source.

Books devoted exclusively to Cumberland County include John A. Oates, *The Story of Fayetteville and the Upper Cape Fear* (Fayetteville: Fayetteville Woman's Club, 1950, and reprinted, 1972); Lucile Miller Johnson, *Hometown Heritage: Fayetteville, North Carolina* (Fayetteville: Colonel Robert Rowan Chapter, National Society Daughters of the American Revolution, 1978); and Harry L. Watson, *Jacksonian Politics and Community Conflict: The Emergence of the Second American Party System in Cumberland County, North Carolina* (Baton Rouge: Louisiana State University Press, 1981). The latter work contains an extensive bibliography of primary and secondary sources for its period.

Histories of various individual church congregations, as well as general histories of Presbyterian, Methodist, and Episcopal denominations in North Carolina, provide information on all periods of Cumberland County history. Two famous men of culture who grew up in Fayetteville left personal journals from the period. They are the artist Elliot Daingerfield (1859-1932) and the pioneering Afro-American novelist and short-story writer Charles Waddell Chesnutt (1858-1932). Typescript copies of journals kept by Daingerfield are in the Cumberland County Public Library; those by Chesnutt are in the Charles Chesnutt Library, Fayetteville State University, Fayetteville.

Collections of photographs in the North Carolina State Archives, the Cumberland County Public Library System, the archival collection in the Charles Chesnutt Library, the 82nd Airborne Division Museum at Fort Bragg, and the library of the Fayetteville Publishing Company are valuable historical sources. A published collection is *Fayetteville, North Carolina: A Pictorial History*, by Weeks Parker (Norfolk, Virginia: Donning Company, 1984).